Into the Darkness: The Harrowing True Story of the Titanic Disaster

Riveting First-Hand Accounts of Agony, Sacrifice and Survival

By Alan J. Rockwell

Bluewave Publishing © 2017

Into the Darkness

Copyright © 2017. All rights reserved. No part of this book may be reproduced in any form or by any means without the prior written permission of the Publisher.

Published by

Bluewave Publishing

Princeton, MN 55371 - USA

Dedicated to the God-inspired human spirit, which enables us to endure, persevere, overcome and even triumph over tragedy.

Table of Contents

INTRODUCTION – An Enduring Fascination

CHAPTER 1 – A Magnificent Engineering Achievement

CHAPTER 2 – Full Steam Ahead

CHAPTER 3 – Heart-wrenching Accounts of Sacrifice, Sorrow and Loss

CHAPTER 4 – Extraordinary Stories of Agony, Horror and Heroism

CHAPTER 5 – Confusion and Panic amid Moments of Calm

CHAPTER 6 – Scenes of Desperation and Despair

CHAPTER 7 – Astonishing Rescues and Emotional Final Moments

CHAPTER 8 – Screams Echo Across a Sea of Glass

CHAPTER 9 – Life and Death Decisions

CHAPTER 10 – Last Goodbyes and Touching Reunions

CHAPTER 11 – *Carpathia* Arrives to a Horrifying Scene

CHAPTER 12 – Criticism of Titanic's Preparedness

CHAPTER 13 – Impending Peril Forces Difficult Choices

CHAPTER 14 – Survivors Recount Terrifying Final Moments

CHAPTER 15 – The Grim Task of Recovery

CHAPTER 16 – Laid to Rest in the Cold, Calm Deep

CHAPTER 17 – Forever Etched into History

INTRODUCTION—An Enduring Fascination

Even though it's been more than a century since the doomed ocean-liner sank beneath the waves to its watery demise, the story of the *Titanic* and its ill-fated maiden voyage still holds a special place in the public eye. It seems people just can't get enough of this story and understandably so—the story of the *Titanic* will most likely always hold the title of the world's largest and deadliest maritime disaster.

There is no one alive today who was actually onboard the *Titanic* that fateful night—all the survivors are dead. For the rest of us, there is very little possibility that the disaster has directly affected us, personally or historically.

And yet, ask people and they will tell you—not just about the iceberg—but probably also about the lifeboats, the "women and children first", and the band playing "Nearer, My God, to Thee" as the ship finally sank with the loss of more than 1,500 lives. The captain, of course, went down with his ship.

But most of all they will tell you about the "unsinkable ship," the biggest and finest ever built, the last word in luxury that sank, seemingly inevitably, on its first and only voyage. They said that "God himself could not sink this ship", but on her maiden voyage she was duly ripped asunder.

When we study popular cultural representations of the *Titanic* in whatever medium, we see the values of the culture, era, and society that made them in vivid reflection. A study of the *Titanic* in British popular culture, for example, reveals distinctly late-Edwardian understandings of race, religion, class and gender, crowned by the captain's much celebrated (but historically unverified) last order to his crew: "Be British!"

The *Titanic* slips consistently in the popular imagination, but the values that go down with it remain many and varied according to the particular perspectives of the tellers of the tale in both time and space.

CHAPTER 1 – A Magnificent Engineering Achievement

The RMS *Titanic* was the largest passenger steamship in the world when she set off on her maiden voyage from Southampton, England, on April 10, 1912. Four days into the trip, on April 14, 1912, she struck an iceberg and sank, resulting in the deaths of 1,517 people.

Having been laid down in 1909, it would take three years of construction and fitting out before RMS *Titanic* was ready for sea. An Olympic-class passenger liner, the *Titanic* was owned by the White Star Line and constructed at the Harland and Wolff shipyard in Belfast, Ireland (now Northern Ireland). She set sail for New York City with 2,223 people on board; the high casualty rate when the ship sank was due in part to the fact that, although complying with the regulations of the time, the ship carried lifeboats for only 1,178 people.

The Titanic was a marvel of engineering achievement, surpassing all her rivals in luxury and extravagance.

The *Titanic* was designed by some of the most experienced engineers, and used some of the most advanced technologies available at the time. It was a great shock to many that, despite the extensive safety features, the *Titanic* sank. The frenzy on the part of the media about the *Titanic*'s famous victims, the legends about the sinking, the resulting changes to maritime law, and the discovery of the wreck have contributed to the interest in the *Titanic*.

The new vessel would forsake speed for the increased safety and comfort that would come with a significant increase in scale. The *Titanic* surpassed all her rivals in luxury and opulence. The first-class section had an on-board swimming pool, a gymnasium, a squash court, Turkish bath, electric bath and a Verandah Cafe. First-class common rooms were adorned with ornate wood paneling, expensive furniture and other decorations. In addition, the Café Parisian offered cuisine for the first-class passengers, with a sunlit veranda fitted with trellis decorations. There were libraries and barber shops in both the first and second-class.

The fascination with RMS *Titanic* is not confined to the lives of her passengers and crew but in the fine technical details about which more is learned all the time. *Titanic* was, on her maiden voyage, the largest vessel afloat. She was 882 feet 9 inches in length and 92 feet in breadth. Her gross tonnage was 46,328 tons. Three propellers were driven by two four-cylinder, triple-expansion, inverted reciprocating steam engines and one low-pressure Parsons turbine. Steam was provided by 25 double-ended and 4 single-ended Scotch-type boilers fired by 159 coal-burning furnaces that gave her a theoretical top speed of 23 knots.

Although she was the largest ship in the world, she was only fractionally greater in size than her sister ship RMS *Olympic*. RMS *Olympic* and RMS

Titanic were constructed side-by-side and less than one year would elapse between their respective maiden voyages. They were practically identical in both appearance and fittings. A third sister, *Britannic*, would follow, but would enter World War One as a vast hospital ship; she would never see service as a passenger liner.

Propellers of the Titanic's sister ship RMS Olympic in dry dock, 1911.

The third class general room had pine paneling and sturdy teak furniture. The ship incorporated technologically advanced features for the period. She had three electric elevators in first class and one in second class. She had also an extensive electrical subsystem with steam-powered generators and ship-wide wiring feeding electric lights and two Marconi radios, including a powerful 1,500-watt set manned by two operators working in shifts, allowing constant contact and the transmission of many passenger messages.

First-class passengers paid a hefty fee for such amenities. The most expensive one-way trans-Atlantic passage was U.S. $4,350 (which is more than U.S. $95,860 in 2008 dollars).

Into the Darkness

The vessel began her maiden voyage with Captain Edward J. Smith in command. As the *Titanic* left her berth, her wake caused the liner SS New York, which was docked nearby, to break away from her moorings, whereupon she was drawn dangerously close (about four feet) to the *Titanic* before a tugboat towed the New York away. The incident delayed departure for about half-an-hour.

Into the Darkness

**Although she was the largest ship in the world, the *Titanic* was only fractionally
greater in size than her sister ship RMS *Olympic*.**

After crossing the English Channel, the *Titanic* stopped at Cherbourg, France, to board additional passengers and stopped again the next day at Queenstown (known today as Cobh), Ireland.

Into the Darkness

As harbor facilities at Queenstown were inadequate for a ship of her size, the *Titanic* had to anchor offshore, with small boats, known as tenders, ferrying the embarking passengers out to her.

CHAPTER 2 – Full Steam Ahead

On the night of Sunday, April 14, 1912, the temperature had dropped to near freezing and the ocean was calm. The moon was not visible (being two days before new moon), and the sky was clear. Captain Smith, in response to iceberg warnings received via wireless over the preceding few days, had drawn up a new course, which took the ship slightly further southward.

That Sunday at 3:45 p.m., a message from the steamer *Amerika* warned that large icebergs lay in the *Titanic*'s path, but as Jack Phillips and Harold Bride, the Marconi wireless radio operators, were employed by Marconi and paid to relay messages to and from the passengers—they were not focused on relaying such "non-essential" ice messages to the bridge.

Into the Darkness

Later that evening, another report of numerous large icebergs, this time from the *Mesaba*, also failed to reach the bridge. At 11:40 p.m., while sailing about 400 miles south of the Grand Banks of Newfoundland, lookouts Fredrick Fleet and Reginald Lee spotted a large iceberg directly ahead of the ship. Fleet sounded the ship's bell three times and telephoned the bridge exclaiming, *"Iceberg, right ahead!"* First Officer Murdoch gave the order "hard-a-starboard", using the traditional tiller order for an abrupt turn to port (left), and adjusted the engines (he either ordered through the telegraph for "full reverse" or "stop" on the engines; (survivor testimony on this differs).

Into the Darkness

Into the Darkness

There was a mighty roar when the ship went down. The bow sank first, with the stern poised in the air, when suddenly it plunged out of sight.

The iceberg brushed the ship's starboard side (right side), buckling the hull in several places and popping out rivets below the waterline over a length of 299 feet (90 m). As seawater filled the forward compartments, the watertight doors shut. However, while the ship could stay afloat with four flooded compartments, five were filling with water.

The five water-filled compartments weighed down the ship so that the tops of the forward watertight bulkheads fell below the ship's waterline, allowing water to pour into additional compartments. Captain Smith, alerted by the jolt of the impact, arrived on the bridge and ordered a full stop. Shortly after midnight on April 15, following an inspection by the ship's officers and Thomas Andrews, the lifeboats were ordered to be readied and a distress call was sent out.

Wireless operators Jack Phillips and Harold Bride were busy sending out CQD, the international distress signal. Several ships responded, including *Mount Temple*, *Frankfurt* and *Titanic*'s sister ship, *Olympic*, but none was close enough to make it in time. The closest ship to respond was Cunard Line's *Carpathia*, 58 miles (93 km) away, which could arrive in an estimated four hours—too late to rescue all of the *Titanic*'s passengers.

The first lifeboat launched was Lifeboat 7 on the starboard side with 28 people on board out of a capacity of 65. It was lowered at around 12:40 a.m., as believed by the British Inquiry. Lifeboat 6 and Lifeboat 5 were launched ten minutes later. Lifeboat 1 was the fifth lifeboat to be launched with 12 people. Lifeboat 11 was overloaded with 70 people. Collapsible D was the last lifeboat to be launched. The *Titanic* carried 20 lifeboats with a total capacity of 1,178 people. While not enough to hold all of the passengers and crew, the *Titanic* carried more boats than was required by the British Board of Trade Regulations. At the time, the number of lifeboats required was determined by a ship's gross register tonnage, rather than her human capacity.

The *Titanic* was given ample stability and sank with only a few degrees list, the design being such that there was very little risk of unequal flooding and possible capsize. Furthermore, the electric power plant was operated by the ship's engineers until the end. Hence, *Titanic* showed no outward signs of being in imminent danger, and passengers were reluctant to leave the apparent safety of the ship to board small lifeboats.

Into the Darkness

Large numbers of third class passengers were unable to reach the lifeboat deck through unfamiliar parts of the ship and past barriers, although some stewards such, as William Denton Cox, successfully led some groups from third class to the lifeboats. As a result, most of the boats were launched partially empty; one boat meant to hold 40 people left the *Titanic* with only 12 people on board.

With "women and children first" the imperative for loading lifeboats, Second Officer Charles Lightoller, who was loading boats on the port side, allowed men to board only if oarsmen were needed, even if there was room. First Officer Murdoch, who was loading boats on the starboard side, let men on board if women were absent. By 2:05 a.m., the entire bow was under water, and all the lifeboats, except for two, had been launched.

Into the Darkness

The final plunge into darkness

Around 2:10, the stern rose out of the water exposing the propellers, and by 2:17 the waterline had reached the boat deck. The last two lifeboats floated off the deck, Collapsible B upside down, Collapsible A half-filled with water, after the supports for its canvas sides were broken in the fall from the roof of the officers' quarters. Shortly afterwards, the forward funnel collapsed, crushing part of the bridge and people in the water. On deck, people were scrambling towards the stern or jumping overboard in hopes of reaching a lifeboat. The ship's stern slowly rose into the air, and everything unsecured crashed towards the water. While the stern rose, the electrical system finally failed and the lights went out.

Shortly afterwards, the stress on the hull caused the *Titanic* to break apart between the last two funnels, and the bow went completely under. The stern righted itself slightly and then rose vertically. After a few moments, at 2:20 a.m., this too sank into the ocean.

Only two of the 18 launched lifeboats rescued people after the ship sank. Lifeboat 4 was close by and picked up five people, two of whom later died. Close to an hour later, Lifeboat 14 went back and rescued four people, one of whom died afterwards. Other people managed to climb onto the lifeboats that floated off the deck. There were some arguments in some of the other lifeboats about going back, but many survivors were afraid of being swamped by people trying to climb into the lifeboat or being pulled down by the suction from the sinking the *Titanic*, though it turned out that there had been very little suction.

As the ship fell into the depths, the two sections behaved very differently. The streamlined bow

Into the Darkness

planed off approximately 2,000 feet (609 m) below the surface and slowed somewhat, landing relatively gently. The stern plunged violently to the ocean floor, the hull being torn apart along the way from massive implosions caused by compression of the air still trapped inside. The stern smashed into the bottom at considerable speed, grinding the hull deep into the silt.

After steaming at 17.5 knots for just under four hours, the RMS *Carpathia* arrived in the area and at 4:10 a.m., began rescuing survivors. By 8:30 she picked up the last lifeboat with survivors and left the area at 8:50 bound for New York.

Of a total of 2,223 people aboard the *Titanic,* only 706 survived the disaster and 1,517 perished. The majority of deaths were caused by hypothermia in the 28 °F (−2 °C) water. At this water temperature, death could be expected in less than 15 minutes.

Men and members of the second and third class were less likely to survive. Of the male passengers in second class, 92 percent perished. Less than half of third-class passengers survived.

Six of the seven children in first class survived, all of the children in second class survived, whereas less than half were saved in third class. Ninety-six percent of the women in first class survived, 86 percent of the women survived in second class and less than half survived in third class. Overall, only 20 percent of the men survived, compared to nearly 75 percent of the women. Men in first class were four times as likely to survive as men in second class, and twice as likely to survive as those in third.

Four of the eight officers survived. About 21 of the 29 able seamen survived and all of the 7 quartermasters and 8 lookouts survived. Three of the 13 leading firemen survived, around 45 other firemen survived and around 20 of the 73 coal trimmers survived. Four of the 33 greasers survived and one of the six mess hall stewards survived. Around 60 of the 322 stewards and 18 of the 23 stewardesses survived. Three of the 68 restaurant staff survived. All of the postal clerks, guarantee group, and eight-member orchestra perished.

Another disparity is that a greater percentage of British passengers died than American passengers; some sources claim this could be because many Britons of the time were polite and queued, rather than forcing their way onto the lifeboats. The captain, Edward John Smith, shouted out: *"Be British, boys, be British!"* as the ocean liner went down, according to witnesses.

CHAPTER 3 – Heart-wrenching Accounts of Sacrifice, Sorrow and Loss

They are all gone now—the *Titanic* survivors. No human being who stood on her decks that night were alive to commemorate the event on its 100th anniversary. Their stories are with us, however, and the lessons remain.

If you could walk the decks of RMS *Titanic* you would hear a dozen or more languages being spoken with every imaginable dialect. Not surprisingly, *Titanic* is often described as a microcosm of society.

On the maiden voyage of the *Titanic*, some of the most prominent people of the day were travelling in first-class. Among them were:

- Millionaire John Jacob Astor IV and his wife Madeleine Force Astor;
- Industrialist Benjamin Guggenheim;
- Macy's owner Isidor Straus and his wife Ida;
- Denver millionairess Margaret "Molly" Brown (known afterwards as the "Unsinkable Molly Brown" due to her efforts in helping other passengers while the ship sank);
- Sir Cosmo Duff Gordon and his wife, couturier Lucy (Lady Duff-Gordon);
- George Dunton Widener, his wife Eleanor, and son Harry;
- Cricketer and businessman John Borland Thayer with his wife Marian and their seventeen-year-old son Jack;
- Journalist William Thomas Stead;
- Lady Countess Rothes (Lucy Noël "Noëlle" Martha Dyer-Edwards), wife of the 19th Earl of Rothes;

- United States presidential aide Archibald Butt;
- Author and socialite Helen Churchill Candee;
- Author Jacques Futrelle his wife May and their friends;
- Broadway producers Henry and Rene Harris and silent film actress Dorothy Gibson, among others. (John Pierpont "J.P." Morgan, an American financier and banker, was scheduled to travel on the maiden voyage, but cancelled at the last minute);
- Travelling in first-class aboard the ship were White Star Line's managing director J. Bruce Ismay and the ship's builder Thomas Andrews, who was on board to observe any problems and assess the general performance of the new ship.

Into the Darkness

The first-class Grand Staircase aboard the *Titanic*.

From the moment the world learned the *Titanic* had sunk, we wanted to know, who had survived? Those answers didn't come until the evening of Thursday, April 18, 1912—when the Cunard liner *Carpathia* finally reached New York with the 706 survivors who had been recovered from *Titanic*'s lifeboats.

Each survivor who descended the gangway had a story to tell—and the world wanted to hear them all.

Into the Darkness

The New York Times sent an army of reporters to fill that need—and gave us stories, such as that from Harold Bride, "*Titanic*'s surviving wireless man." The junior operator relayed the story of the ship's band. "The way the band kept playing was a noble thing. I heard it first while still we were working wireless when there was a ragtime tune for us, and the last I saw of the band, when I was floating out in the sea with my lifebelt on, it was still on deck playing 'Autumn.' How they ever did it I cannot imagine."

There were stories of heroism—such as that of Edith Evans, who was waiting to board Collapsible D, the last boat to leave *Titanic*, when she turned to Caroline Brown and said, "You go first. You have children waiting at home." The sacrifice cost Evans her life, but as Mrs. Brown said later, "It was a heroic sacrifice, and as long as I live I shall hold her memory dear as my preserver, who preferred to die so that I might live."

There was cowardice. Most men who survived found themselves trying to explain how they survived when women and children had died, but most of this vitriol was directed at White Star Chairman J. Bruce Ismay, who survived the sinking of the ship he had commissioned. Ostracized by society and haunted by negative press, Ismay remained a virtual recluse for the rest of his life and died at age 74 in 1937.

There was mystery. Two little French boys had been placed aboard Collapsible D by their father, known to those on board as "Mr. Hoffman." Having lost their father, and not being able to speak English or explain who they were, the boys became known as "The *Titanic* Waifs" in photographs that were carried in newspapers worldwide. Their mother

Into the Darkness

back in France recognized her sons and sailed to New York to reclaim them. The boys' father, whose real name was Michel Navratil, had been in the midst of a bitter divorce and had abducted the boys before boarding *Titanic*.

Mostly, there was loss. On her return to New York after picking up *Titanic*'s survivors, *Carpathia* had become known as a ship of widows. Rene Harris, who lost her husband, Broadway producer Henry Harris, in the disaster, later spoke of her loss when she said, "It was not a night to remember. It was a night to forget."

More than one hundred years after the RMS *Titanic* met its fatal end, the story of the tragic wreck continues to fascinate people worldwide. Though many survivors and their family members disappeared into obscurity or were hesitant to talk about what they went through, others were willing to share their experiences during the wreck and in its aftermath. These are some of their stories.

Ellen Shine

A thrilling story was told by Ellen Shine, a 20-year-old girl from County Cork, Ireland, who crossed to America to visit her brother.

"Those who were able to get out of bed," said Miss Shine, "rushed to the upper deck where they were met by members of the crew who endeavored to keep them in the steerage quarters.

"The women however rushed past the men and finally reached the upper deck. When they were informed that the boat was sinking, most of them fell on their knees and began to pray. I saw one of the lifeboats and made for it.

"In it there were already four men from the steerage who refused to obey an officer who ordered them out. They were, however, finally turned out."

Into the Darkness

That report, carried in *The Times of London* on Saturday April 20 is exactly the same as quotes attributed to Ellen Shine and carried in the *Denver Post*, the *Daily Times*, and other U.S. newspapers on the previous day, with one difference. The American reports continued:

"… in it were four men from the steerage. They were ordered out by an officer and refused to leave. And then one of the officers jumped into the boat, and, drawing a revolver, shot the four men dead. Their bodies were picked out from the bottom of the boat and thrown into the ocean."

How can posterity reconcile these two versions? Were the claimed killings the product of a survivor's fevered mind or a journalist's reckless embellishment? Did Reuters (news agency) deliberately choose to tone down the story in plucking it from another source, or was there simply no mention by Ellen of any killings in the first place?

Into the Darkness

No other witnesses described four men being callously shot inside a lifeboat by an officer of the White Star Line, and no bodies were ever recovered with discernible gunshot wounds.

Ellen Shine appears to have escaped in Lifeboat No. 13, which was located as the second-last boat on the starboard side, towards the stern. Eugene Daly frankly confesses that he was a steerage passenger who climbed into a lifeboat in defiance of orders at this location. Daly said he was forced from a boat at the 'second cabin deck', an area of promenade for middle-ranking passengers, and talks of being on the starboard side, where boat No. 13 was lowering:

"We afterwards went to the second cabin deck and the two girls and myself got into a boat. An officer called on me to go back, but I would not stir. Then they got a hold of me and pulled me out."

Into the Darkness

No one testified to any disorder at boat No. 13 at the two official inquiries. Steward Frederick Ray, who was in this boat, told the U.S. Senate investigators, in reply to questions, that he saw no male passengers or men of the crew "ordered out or thrown out of these lifeboats on the starboard side. Everybody was very orderly." But Irish passenger Dannie Buckley declared:

"Time and again officers would drag men from the boats." Resolution of the problem is elusive. Should one disregard the claims of men shot dead for staying stubbornly in a lifeboat? Someone somewhere is spinning pure invention.

Ellen Shine told her story once and would never be drawn on it again. According to the embarkation records, she was an 18-year-old spinster, but by the time U.S. immigration had come aboard the *Carpathia*, she declared herself to be a 16-year-old servant from County Cork. She was actually aged

17 when she boarded the *Titanic* and from the small hamlet of Lisrobin. She was on her way to join her brother Jeremiah in New York.

Shine collapsed in hysterics when met by Jeremiah and other relatives at the Cunard pier in New York, according to the *Brooklyn Daily* Eagle. It reported the next day that she and other women had knocked down crewmen who tried to prevent steerage passengers from reaching the boat deck.

Ellen Shine Callaghan died on March 5, 1993, and is buried in St Charles Cemetery, East Farmingdale, New York.

Millvina Dean

The last known survivor of the *Titanic* disaster was Elizabeth Gladys Millvina Dean, known as Millvina.

Millvina Dean

Millvina was just two months old when she sailed on the *Titanic* with her parents when they decided to leave England for America back in 1912. Her father had planned to open a tobacco shop when he arrived. Unfortunately her father never made it off *Titanic* that night and his body, if recovered, was never identified.

"Nobody knew about me and the *Titanic*, to be honest, nobody took any interest, so I took no interest either," Dean said. "But then they found the wreck, and after they found the wreck, they found me."

For the last two decades of her life, Dean attended *Titanic* conventions and granted interviews in which she talked about the tragedy that had claimed her father so many years before. She refused to see James Cameron's *Titanic* for fear of memories it would stir about her father. "It would have made me think, did he jump overboard or did he go down with the ship?" she said. "I would have been very emotional."

Into the Darkness

The Dean family was not originally meant to be on board *Titanic*. They had been transferred to the ship along with a few other passengers because of the cancellation of another ship due to a coal strike.

Millvina, her brother and her mother left the ship safely on board Lifeboat 10 and were rescued by the *Carpathia* a few hours later. After the disaster, the family returned to England, where Millvina lived the rest of her life. Her mother died in 1975, aged 96; and her brother died in 1992, aged 81.

Millvina had been a star from the moment she was brought aboard *Carpathia*, where women clamored to hold "this lovable mite of humanity," and when she died at age 97 on May 31, 2009, the 98th anniversary of the *Titanic*'s launch, we lost our last living link to the *Titanic*.

Ruth Elizabeth Becker

Ruth Elizabeth Becker, known later as Ruth Becker Blanchard, was one of the youngest passengers on the *Titanic* at 12 years old, and until relatively recently, was one of the few remaining *Titanic* survivors. Her story is harrowing, but it's inspirational that someone so young was able to exhibit such bravery, even in the face of a horrific disaster that few of us can truly picture in our minds.

The daughter of a Lutheran missionary, Ruth was born in Guntur, India in 1899. When her brother became ill, her mother Nellie decided to take him and the rest of the family to Benton Harbor, Michigan for medical treatment. Ruth, her mother, and her younger brother and sister boarded the RMS *Titanic* as second-class passengers, with her father waiting behind in India to rejoin them later.

Into the Darkness

Ruth and her family marveled at the beauty and grandeur of the ship, but their trip took a nasty turn when disaster struck. Ruth's mother managed to get into Lifeboat No. 11 with her two youngest children, but there was no room left for Ruth. Nellie sobbed as she was separated from her daughter, who ended up in Lifeboat No. 13.

As Ruth's lifeboat was lowered into the water, it was very nearly crushed by Lifeboat No. 15, which was being lowered too quickly. A crew member managed to cut the ropes binding No. 13 to the ship at the last minute, and the boat slid away in the nick of time. The air was filled with the chilling sound of screams from those stranded in the icy water. A young Polish woman in Ruth's lifeboat lamented her missing baby, who had been separated from her much like Ruth had been separated from her family. Though she didn't understand German, Ruth did her best to comfort the upset mother.

Finally, the lifeboat was rescued by the RMS *Carpathia*. After several tense hours of waiting and dreading the worst, Ruth was overjoyed to see her mother and siblings alive and well. She was also happy to discover that the Polish woman from her lifeboat had been reunited with her baby.

Ruth refused to talk about the traumatic *Titanic* sinking incident for many years. Later, she began to talk more about it, and made appearances at *Titanic* Historical Society conventions along with other *Titanic* survivors.

In 1990, Ruth Becker Blanchard took a cruise to Mexico, her first time as a passenger on a ship since the *Titanic* disaster. She died later that year at the age of 90, and her ashes were scattered at sea, directly over the *Titanic* wreck.

In an astonishing incident of luck and coincidence, one of the most amazing stories of any *Titanic* survivors comes from Violet Constance Jessop, an ocean liner stewardess and a nurse who survived the sinking of both the RMS *Titanic* in 1912 and the HMHS *Britannic* and 1916. Even more amazingly, she had been aboard the *Britannic's* other sister ship the RMS *Olympic* when it nearly sank after colliding with the naval vessel, the HMS *Hawke* in 1911.

Margaret "Molly" Brown

One of the most prominent *Titanic* survivors was Margaret "Molly" Brown (Margaret Tobin). On several occasions Mrs. Brown has been referred to as one of the heroines of the *Titanic* disaster. She and her family preferred to say merely that she was "a survivor." She was rescued by the *Carpathia* after spending seven hours in one of the *Titanic's* boats, doing her share at the oars.

Into the Darkness

After the ship struck the iceberg, Margaret helped load others into lifeboats and eventually was forced to board Lifeboat 6. She and the other women in Lifeboat 6 worked together to row, keep spirits up, and dispel the gloom that was broadcast by the emotional and unstable Robert Hichens.

However, Margaret's most significant work occurred on *Carpathia*, where she assisted *Titanic* survivors, and afterwards in New York. By the time *Carpathia* reached New York harbor, Margaret had helped establish the Survivor's Committee, been elected as chair, and raised almost $10,000 for destitute survivors. Margaret's language skills in French, German, and Russian were an asset, and she remained on *Carpathia* until all *Titanic* survivors had met with friends, family, or medical/emergency assistance. In a letter to her daughter shortly after the *Titanic* sinking, she wrote:

Into the Darkness

"After being brined, salted, and pickled in mid ocean I am now high and dry... I have had flowers, letters, telegrams, and people until I am befuddled. They are petitioning Congress to give me a medal... If I must call a specialist to examine my head it is due to the title of Heroine of the Titanic."

Her sense of humor prevailed; to her attorney in Denver she wired: "Thanks for the kind thoughts. Water was fine and swimming good. Neptune was exceedingly kind to me and I am now high and dry."

On May 29, 1912, as chair of the Survivor's Committee Margaret presented a silver loving cup to Captain Rostron of the *Carpathia* and a medal to each *Carpathia* crew member. In later years, Margaret helped erect the *Titanic* memorial that stands in Washington, D.C.; visited the cemetery in Halifax, Nova Scotia, to place wreaths on the graves of victims; and continued to serve on the Survivor's Committee. She was particularly upset that, as a woman, she was not allowed to testify at the *Titanic* hearings. In response, she wrote her own version of the event, which was published in newspapers in Denver, New York, and Paris.

Molly Brown with Captain Rostron of the *Carpathia*

Charles Joughin

One of the most renowned *Titanic* survivor stories is that of Charles Joughin—the man who somehow drank his way through the *Titanic* disaster and lived to tell the tale. Here is an account of his bizarre story that some still find hard to swallow.

Like any cruise ship of current times, the *Titanic* was designed as one big party boat. You can't go on a cruise ship without entertaining the idea of having a few cocktails to go along with the view, and the *Titanic* was no different. According to the ship's manifest, the drink order for the *Titanic* included 1,500 bottles of wine, 15,000 champagne glasses, 20,000 bottles of beer and stout, and at least 850 bottles of spirits. The cargo manifest reveals further reserves of 17 cases of cognac, 70 cases of wine and 191 cases of liquor. This was all in addition to the personal stocks of booze that passengers were sure to have included as well.

Into the Darkness

In addition to the copious amounts of spirits that were aboard the *Titanic*, there were also a variety of drinking and smoking rooms. This translated into the *Titanic* being roughly a paradise of drinking and debauchery. Some sources speak of passengers making quips pertaining to ice after the *Titanic* struck the iceberg in the middle of the North Atlantic, but none of these have actually been recorded or confirmed. The *Titanic* ultimately did sink, but *Titanic* survivor Charles Joughin and his friend, alcohol, lived to tell the tale.

Into the Darkness

Charles Joughin

Depicted in both "A night to Remember" and the 1997 blockbuster *"Titanic"* movie, Charles Joughin is shown as the drunk guy hanging onto the side of the rail. Many individuals may only see the character as a commentary on a certain outlook on the sinking *Titanic*, but this character actually survived the disaster by warming his insides with whiskey. Those who documented the story of Joughin cite alcohol as one of the contributors to his survival. Along with this cool headed approach to the situation, documents illustrate that the chef survived longer in the icy Atlantic as a direct result of his blood alcohol level.

During the sinking of the *Titanic*, Joughin and the other chefs were tasked with bringing food and supplies to put aboard the lifeboats. Many depictions of Joughin fail to submit this fact and focus more on his excessive drinking. After awaiting his fate in his cabin while hitting the bottle, Joughin ventured onto the top deck and began helping people onto lifeboats and declining to board one himself. Returning to his cabin and further fortifying himself for another half hour, Joughin would later emerge to throw chairs and other items overboard in hopes to give those who fell overboard something to hang onto.

Into the Darkness

After the *Titanic* had completely been submerged, the story cites that Joughin stepped off of the stern of the ship without as much as getting his hair wet. Accounts say that he survived three hours (although the length of time is debated) in the freezing Atlantic. Some say that this was a result of the amount of alcohol in his blood, and others have different explanations. No matter how the details read, the fact is that Joughin survived the sinking of the *Titanic* and managed to keep a level head during the entire disaster.

His heroism under the influence has gone all but unnoticed over the years. Joughin died at age 78 in 1956 in Patterson, New Jersey.

Eva Miriam Hart

Eva Hart was seven years old when she and her parents boarded the *Titanic* as second-class passengers at Southampton, England. They had originally been booked on a ship called the *Philadelphia*, but the coal strike at Southampton that spring kept it from sailing and many of her passengers were transferred to the *Titanic*. Almost instantly, her mother felt uneasy about the *Titanic* and feared that some catastrophe would happen. To call a ship unsinkable was, in her mind, flying in the face of God. With such fear, she slept only during the day and stayed awake in their cabin at night fully dressed.

Eva was sleeping when the *Titanic* struck the iceberg at 11:40 p.m. on April 14. Her father rushed into their cabin to alert her and her mother, and after wrapping her in a blanket, he carried her to the boat deck. He placed his wife and daughter in Lifeboat

Into the Darkness

14 and told Eva to "be a good girl and hold Mommy's hand." It was the last thing he ever said to her and the last time she ever saw him.

She and her mother were picked up by the rescue ship RMS *Carpathia* and arrived in New York City on April 18. Her father perished and his body, if recovered, was never identified.

Eva and Esther Hart (center and right) upon their return to England after the sinking of the *Titanic*.

Soon after arriving in America, she and her mother returned to England and the latter remarried. She was plagued with nightmares and upon the death of her mother in 1928 when Hart was 23, she confronted her fears head-on by returning to the sea and locking herself in a cabin for four straight days until the nightmares went away.

Eva Hart died on February 14, 1996 at her home in Chadwell Heath, London, two weeks after her 91st birthday. Her death left eight remaining survivors.

Chapter 4 — Extraordinary Stories of Agony, Horror and Heroism

One of the more heart-wrenching first-hand accounts came in the form of a letter written by a French woman name Rose Amelie Icard. The letter is dated August 8, 1955—more than 40 years after the disaster. In the letter, Icard describes the "horror" and "sublime heroism" of passengers assisting others as the stricken vessel vanished to the depths of the ocean.

The survivor also tells of still suffering from nightmares 43 years on. She wrote: "Towards eleven o'clock, Mrs. Stone and I went to bed. Three quarters of an hour later, as the liner was cruising at full speed, a terrifying shock threw us out of bed."

"We were intending to find out what was happening, when a passing officer told us 'It is nothing, return to your cabin.' I answered 'Listen to that loud noise, it sounds like water is flowing into the ship.'"

Their luxury cruise turned into a desperate bid to escape the "unsinkable ship," which was now flooding with water. Incredibly Ms. Icard almost became trapped in the depths after trying to go retrieve Mrs. Stone's precious jewelry.

She wrote: "We felt beneath our feet the deck lean towards the depths. I went back below decks to retrieve the jewels of Mrs. Stone. I choose the wrong stairwell and returned to the deck halfway there.

"Fortunately for me, for I would have never come back up again. At this moment we witnessed unforgettable scenes of horror mixed with the most sublime heroism."

Into the Darkness

"Women, still in evening gowns, some just out of bed, barely clothed, disheveled, distraught, scrambled for the boats. Commander Smith yelled, 'Women and children first'."

"Firm and calm, in the throng, officers and sailors were taking the women and children by the arm and directing them towards the lifeboats."

There were some moments of heartbreaking drama and displays of love during the last moments of *Titanic* and its doomed passengers. As frightened wives were being placed in lifeboats, while their husbands stayed on the sinking liner, they screamed for a final unity.

Ms. Icard wrote: "Near me were two handsome elderly people, Mr. and Mrs. Straus, proprietors of the great store Macy's of New York.

"She refused to go into the boat after having helped in her maid.

"She put her arms around the neck of her husband, telling him: 'We have been married 50 years, we have never left each other; I want to die with you.'"

"Semi-conscious, in a neighboring boat was put the young wife of the millionaire J. Jacob Astor, returning from their honeymoon voyage, she was 20 years old, him 50.

"She latches on to him, he was obliged to push her away with force.

"There had been sublime gestures; a stranger undid his safety belt to give it to an old woman who couldn't find a spot in any boat, and told her 'You'll pray for me.'"

Into the Darkness

The maid also gives dramatic details of how she rowed to relative safety in the freezing waters as the *Titanic* was swallowed by the Atlantic.

"Suddenly, there was darkness, whole and inscrutable, shouts, horrible yells, rose in the middle of the creaks of the boat, then that was it," she wrote.

"Sometimes, 43 years after the tragedy, I still dream about it."

Before the surviving passengers were picked up from the lifeboats by the *Carpathia* and taken to New York, the vessel returned to the spot where *Titanic* went down.

In vivid detail, Icard described the scene: "The waters were calm and bare, and nothing could suggest that the sea giant was engulfed there.

"Alone, in front of us, two cathedrals of ice, which were pinkening under the first sunlight, offered a spectacle of rare beauty."

Ms. Icard died in July 1964, nearly 10 years after the letter was released.

William E. Carter

William E. Carter, along with his wife and two children, Lucille and William E. Carter, Jr., were among those saved from the wreck of the *Titanic*. In the same lifeboat with Mrs. Carter and her two children were the three women most notable among the survivors. They were Mrs. John Jacob Astor, Mrs. George D. Widener and Mrs. John B. Thayer.

Colonel Astor, Mr. Thayer, Mr. Widener and Mr. Carter separated as soon as the ladies were safely in the lifeboats, and Mr. Carter never saw the three men again.

Mr. Carter was a passenger on the lifeboat in which J. Bruce Ismay, managing director of the White Star Line, made his escape from the sinking liner. Mr. Carter declared that the boat was the last to leave the starboard side of the *Titanic* and was nearly the last which left the vessel.

When entered by Mr. Carter and Mr. Ismay, the boat was occupied entirely by women of the third cabin. Every woman on the starboard side of the vessel had been sent off in lifeboats when he and Mr. Ismay got into the boat, Mr. Carter said.

Mr. Carter expressed the greatest admiration for the discipline maintained by the officers of the *Titanic*, and voiced the opinion that Mr. Ismay should not be held open to criticism.

Into the Darkness

"If there had been another woman to go, neither Mr. Ismay nor myself would have gotten into the boat. There can be no criticism of Mr. Ismay's action."

In describing his experience, Mr. Carter said he had urged Harry Widener to go with him to the starboard side of the vessel. Young Mr. Widener, thinking that there was no immediate danger, remarked that he would take his chances on the vessel.

Mr. Carter said he was in the smoking room of the *Titanic* when the crash came. "I was talking to Major Butt, Clarence Moore and Harry Widener," he explained. "It was just seventeen minutes to 12 o'clock.

"Although there was quite a jar, I thought the trouble was slight. I believe it was the immense size of the *Titanic,* which brought many of the passengers to believe there was no danger. I went on deck to see what had happened. Almost as I reached the deck, the engines were stopped."

Mr. Carter continued: "I hurried down to see about my family and found they were all in bed. Just then the vessel listed a little to port, and I told my wife and children they had better get up and dress.

"Just then, orders were issued for everyone to get on life preservers. When we came out on the deck, boats were being lowered. Mrs. Carter and the children got into the fourth or fifth boat with Mrs. Astor, Mrs. Widener and Mrs. Thayer.

"After I got my family into the boat and saw it pushed off, the *Titanic* listed more and more to one side. I decided that I had better look out for myself and went up to a deck on the starboard side. In the meantime a good many boats were getting off.

Into the Darkness

"There were no women on the starboard side when I reached there except one collapsible raft load of third-class women passengers. Mr. Ismay and myself got into the boat, which was either the last or the next to the last to leave the *Titanic*.

"As we left the ship, the lights went out and the *Titanic* started to go down. The crash had ripped up the side and the water rushing into the boiler-room caused the boilers to explode," Carter said.

"We were a good distance off when we saw the *Titanic* dip and disappear. We stayed in the boat until about 5 o'clock, Mr. Ismay and myself pulling on the oars with three members of the crew practically all the time.

"Never in my life have I seen such splendid discipline as was maintained by Captain Smith and his men. There was no panic and the order was splendid.

"Before I left Harry Widener, I urged him to come with me to the starboard side of the ship, and it was then he told me he would take his chances on the vessel. He had on a life belt, as did every other passenger, many of whom stayed in the smoking room playing bridge.

"I saw Colonel Astor place his wife in the same boat that put my family in, and at the same time Mr. Widener parted from his wife and Mr. Thayer put Mrs. Thayer in the boat. I did not see the men again."

The ship was loaded with only enough lifeboats to hold half of the *Titanic* passengers.

John Jacob Astor

The heroism of the majority of the men who went down to death with the *Titanic* has been told over and over again. How John Jacob Astor kissed his wife and saluted death as he looked squarely into its face; the devotion of Mrs. Isidor Straus to her aged husband and the willingness with which she went to her room with his loving arms pressed tenderly around her; the tales of life sacrificed that women might be saved brought some need of comfort to the stricken.

Into the Darkness

G.A. Brayton, of Los Angeles, Cal., says: "John Jacob Astor went to one of the officers and told them who he was, and asked to go in the lifeboat with his wife. The officer told him he could not go in the lifeboat. Astor then kissed his wife good-bye and she was put in the lifeboat. Astor said: 'I resign myself to my fate' and saluted in farewell.

"Colonel Astor and Major Archibald Butt died together on the bridge of the ill-fated ship," said Dr. Washington Dodge, of San Francisco, one of the survivors. "I saw them standing here side by side. I was in one of the last boats, and I could not mistake them. Earlier during the desperate struggle to get the boats cleared, I had seen them both at work quieting passengers and helping the officers maintain order.

"A few minutes before the last I saw Colonel Astor help his wife, who appeared ill, into a boat, I saw him wave his hand to her and smile as the boat pulled away."

Before the lifeboats left the ship, not far from the woman who would not let her husband meet death alone, Colonel Astor stood supporting the figure of his young bride, says another survivor. A boat was being filled with women. Colonel Astor helped his wife to a place in it. The boat was not filled, and there seemed no more women near it. Quietly the Colonel turned to the second officer, who was superintending the loading.

"May I go with my wife? She is ill," he asked. The officer nodded. The man of millions got into the boat. The crew were about to cast off the falls. Suddenly the Colonel sprang to his feet, shouting to them to wait. He had seen a woman running toward the boat. Leaping over the rail, he helped her to the place he had occupied.

Into the Darkness

Mrs. Astor screamed and tried to climb from the boat. The Colonel restrained her. He bent and tenderly patted her shoulder.

"The ladies first, dear heart," he was heard to say.

Then quietly he saluted the second officer and turned to help in lowering more boats.

A nephew of Senator Clark, of Butte, Montana, said Astor stood by the after rail looking after the lifeboats until the *Titanic* went down.

Brayton says: "Captain Smith stood on the bridge until he was washed off by a wave. He swam back, stood on the bridge again and was there when the *Titanic* went to the bottom."

Brayton says that Henry B. Harris, the theatrical manager, tried to get on a lifeboat with his wife, but the second officer held him back with a gun. "A third-class passenger who tried to climb in the boats was shot and killed by a steward. This was the only shooting on board I know of."

Into the Darkness

Captain Edward J. Smith

Captain Edward J. Smith died a hero's death. He went to the bottom of the ocean without effort to save himself. His last acts were to place a five-year-old child on the last lifeboat in reach, then cast his life belt to the ice ridden waters and resigned to the fate that tradition down the ages observed as a strict law.

Captain Edward J. Smith, Captain of the Titanic

Into the Darkness

It was left to a fireman of the *Titanic* to tell the tale of the death of Captain Smith and the last message he left behind him. This man had gone down with the vessel and was clinging to a piece of wreckage about half an hour before he finally joined several members of the *Titanic*'s company on the bottom of a boat which was floating among other wreckage.

Harry Senior, the fireman, with his eight or nine companions in distress, had just managed to get a firm hold on the upturned boat, when they saw the *Titanic* rearing preparatory to her final plunge. At that moment, according to the fireman's tale, Captain Smith jumped into the sea from the promenade deck of the *Titanic* with an infant clutched tenderly in his arms.

It only took a few strokes to bring him to the upturned lifeboat, where a dozen hands were stretched out to take the little child from his arms and drag him to safety.

"Captain Smith was dragged on the upturned boat," said the fireman. "He had on a life buoy and a life preserver. He clung there a moment and then he slid off again. For a second time he was dragged from the icy water. Then he took off his life preserver, tossed the life buoy on the inky waters and slipped into the water again with the words: 'I will follow the ship.'"

At that time there was only a circle of troubled water and some wreckage to show the spot where the biggest of all ocean steamers had sunk out of sight.

"No," said the stoker, as he waved a sandwich above his head, holding a glass of beer in the other hand, "Captain Smith never shot himself. I saw what he did. He went down with that ship. I'll stake my life on that."

Robert M. Daniel

Captain Smith was a guest at a banquet which was being given by W. Bruce Ismay, managing director of the White Star Line, when the big steamer plunged into that fated iceberg, according to Robert M. Daniel, member of the banking firm of Hillard-Smith, Daniel & Co. of Philadelphia.

The fourth officer was in charge of the vessel, said Mr. Daniel. "We were about fifty miles ahead of our schedule at the time the accident happened," said Mr. Daniel, "and were running at about a twenty-mile-an-hour rate. Everybody on board had been talking all along about how we were trying to beat the *Olympic's* record for the Western trip and many pools were made on each day's run.

"I was asleep in my berth when the collision came and so cannot tell how we happened to hit that berg or what occurred immediately afterwards. I got up and looked out of my stateroom door; but all seemed to be quiet and I went back to bed again.

"A little later I heard someone crying that the boats were being manned and I got frightened. So I wrapped an overcoat about me and went on deck. On the way I grabbed a life belt and tied it on."

Mr. Daniel continued: "The boat had already sunk so far down that the lower decks were awash. I didn't waste any time in thinking. I just jumped overboard. I clung to the same overturned lifeboat that young John B. Thayer, Jr., swam to later and saw him jump from the *Titanic*. It looked to me as though his father pushed him off and jumped after him, but the boat sank so soon afterwards and things were so mixed up that I couldn't be sure about that.

"A boat came by after a while that was full of women. They were frightened and seeing me, pulled me aboard, saying they needed a man to take charge. I did my best to cheer them up, but it was a poor effort and didn't succeed very well. Still I kept them busy with one thing and another and so helped pass the weary hours until we were picked up by the *Carpathia*."

Mr. Daniel stated with emphasis that Colonel John Jacob Astor stayed on the *Titanic* until the last second, then jumped just as the liner was going down, and he did not see the millionaire again.

Captain Smith also stuck to the bridge, until the ship sank, said Mr. Daniel, when the skipper also jumped, but disappeared below the waves and apparently never came up again.

"I spoke to the fourth officer just before I went to my cabin," said Mr. Daniel, "and he told me he was in charge while the captain was at dinner. Then I remembered I had heard Ismay was giving a banquet.

"The fourth officer said the skipper was coming up 'pretty soon' to relieve him," added Mr. Daniel.

On the *Carpathia*, Mr. Daniel said, were 19 women who had been made widows by the *Titanic* disaster. Six of them were young brides who were returning on the steamship from honeymoon trips.

While on the *Carpathia*, Mr. Daniel proved of considerable assistance to the wireless operator. He was an amateur student of wireless telegraphy. Following the disaster, the operator on the *Carpathia* was compelled to work night and day.

While the operator was engaged in the arduous task of sending to shore the long list of those who had been snatched from the sea, Mr. Daniel went into the operating room. He found the operator on the verge of collapse, and, volunteering his services, sent a large part of the list himself.

Mr. Daniel denied that all the lifeboats and collapsible rafts launched from the *Titanic* had been picked up by the *Carpathia*.

"Only 12 boats were picked up," he said, "while there were half a dozen more that drifted away in other directions. There has been no storm, and I don't see why they should not have been located by some other vessel."

A German steamer, the *Frankfurt*, was 35 miles nearer to the *Titanic* than was the *Carpathia* at the time of the accident, but for some reason would not come to the assistance of the stricken liner, Mr. Daniel said.

Asked if any women had been left aboard the *Titanic* he said: "Only those women who positively refused to leave their husbands and who could not be forced into lifeboats for lack of time.

"One of the most remarkable features of this horrible affair is the length of time that elapsed after the collision before the seriousness of the situation dawned on the passengers. The officers assured everybody that there was no danger, and we all had such confidence in the *Titanic* that it didn't occur to anybody that she might sink," Mr. Daniel said.

As to the reports that many persons had been shot to prevent them from rushing the lifeboats, Mr. Daniel said several shots had been fired in the air to frighten the steerage passengers and keep them in order, but that he did not know or hear of anyone being hit by a bullet.

Mrs. John Jacob Astor, said Mr. Daniel, had been confined to her stateroom under the doctor's care during her stay on the *Carpathia*. "I did not lay eyes on her nor on Bruce Ismay. He stuck close to his cabin and I don't think he came on deck once during the trip on the *Carpathia*."

Even when the passengers finally realized that the *Titanic* was doomed, there was no disorder, according to Mr. Daniel. The crew's discipline was perfect and the women were placed in the boats quietly and without confusion. It was only after the ship had gone down, he added, and the women awoke to the fact that their husbands, brothers, sons and sweethearts, who had told them they would follow "in other boats," had sunk to their death, that there was any hysteria, he said.

Mr. Daniel continued: "Then the cries were awful to listen to; some of the women screamed all the time. For four straight hours they kept at it. First from one boat, then from another. It was heart-rending."

Asked why the *Carpathia* had refused to answer the wireless messages relayed to her, Mr. Daniel answered that so many land stations were trying to get the vessel that the air was full of cross currents, and it was almost impossible to catch any one message meant for the rescue ship, let alone trying to reply to any of them.

While Mr. Daniel was talking to the newspaper men on the pier, just after landing from the *Carpathia*, a man ran up and, showing him two newspaper photographs, asked if he remembered the face.

"It's my brother, Mr. White, of California," said the man. "Is he on board the *Carpathia*?"

"I don't think so," answered Mr. Daniel. "I remember meeting this gentleman on board the *Titanic*, but I have not seen him since." Mr. White's brother grabbed the photographs and rushed away.

Into the Darkness

Many of the men, said Mr. Daniel, refused to jump from the *Titanic* until the ship was actually disappearing beneath the waves.

"They seemed to think they were safer on board," he said, "and by waiting too long lost their chance of being saved for they were probably carried down by the suction. Howard B. Case, of New York, was one who declined to jump. C. Duane Williams was another. He was washed overboard, but his son, Richard Norris Williams, jumped and was saved."

Mr. Daniel was in the water or on a cake of ice nearly an hour before he was pulled aboard a lifeboat. He had nothing to keep him from freezing save a light overcoat over his pajamas. While on the *Carpathia*, he slept on the floor of the dining saloon and was so weak when he landed that he could hardly move.

Mr. Daniel describes his final leap: "When I finally went on deck," he said, "the water already was up to my ankles. I saw the women and some of the men taking to the boats. A short distance away was a big cake of ice. I jumped for it and crawled on it.

"John B. Thayer, Jr., came to the same ice cake later, after the *Titanic* sank. Then a boat passed near and he swam to it and was pulled aboard. A half hour afterwards, another boat came by and I was pulled aboard.

"It seemed a long time before we saw the masts of the *Carpathia*, but when the straight masts and the blur of smoke from her funnels were outlined against the horizon, we realized that it meant rescue for all of us. When the boat finally reached us, the men in the boat did what they could to help the women to the vessel, but most of us were almost helpless from the cold and exposure.

"I cannot pretend to explain the accident. All I can say is that we knew for five hours before the accident that there were ice fields about. I saw Colonel Astor after I was on the raft. He was still on deck. The water was washing about his knees. He made no effort to get into a boat.

"The last I saw of Major Butt [United States presidential aide Archibald Butt]," Mr. Daniel added, "he was playing bridge with Clarence Moore, of Washington, and two other men. This was just before I went to my cabin.

"When I came on deck again, I did not see him. I have no doubt he met his death as a soldier should."

Into the Darkness

Archibald Butt

From the moment the *Titanic* climbed to her death on the jagged shelf of the great iceberg until the last boatload of women and children, and some men, was lowered, United States presidential aide Major Archibald Butt was, to all intents and purposes, an officer not only of the American Army, but of the British mercantile marine. He was among the first to realize the gravity of the *Titanic*'s condition, and he immediately forgot himself and went to the assistance of the sorely taxed skipper and junior officers of the sinking liner.

He was here and there and everywhere, giving words of encouragement to weeping women and children, and uttering when necessary commands to keep the weak-kneed men from giving in and rendering the awful situation even more terrible.

Captain Charles E. Crain, of the 27th United States Infantry was a passenger on the *Carpathia*, and when he learned that Major Butt was among the dead, he made it his duty to get the true tale of his comrade's death.

"Butt, I was told, was as cool as the iceberg that had doomed the ship, and not once did he lose control of himself. In the presence of death he was the same gallant, courteous officer that the American people had learned to know so well as a result of his constant attendance upon President Taft. There was never any chance of Butt getting into any of those lifeboats.
"He knew his time was at hand, and he was ready to meet it as a man should, and I, and all of the others who cherish his memory, are glad that he faced the situation that way, which was the only possible way a man of his caliber could face it."

Mrs. Henry B. Harris, of Washington, a survivor of the *Titanic*, said: "That man's conduct will remain in my memory forever; the way he showed some of the other men how to behave when women and children were suffering that awful mental fear that came when we had to be huddled in those boats. Major Butt was near me, and I know very nearly everything he did."

Chapter 5 — Confusion and Panic amid Moments of Calm

One of the more compelling accounts of events of that night came from Dr. Washington Dodge of San Francisco:

"We had retired to our stateroom, and the noise of the collision was not at all alarming. We had just fallen asleep. My wife awakened me and said that something had happened to the ship. We went on deck and everything seemed quiet and orderly.

"The orchestra was playing a lively tune. They started to lower the lifeboats after a lapse of some minutes. There was little excitement.

"As the lifeboats were being launched, many of the first-cabin passengers expressed their preference of staying on the ship. The passengers were constantly being assured that there was no danger, but that as a matter of extra precaution, the women and children should be placed in the lifeboats," Dodge said.

"Everything was still quiet and orderly when I placed Mrs. Dodge and the boy in the fourth or fifth boat. I believe there were 20 boats lowered away altogether. I did what I could to help in keeping order, as after the sixth or seventh boat was launched, the excitement began.

"Some of the passengers fought with such desperation to get into the lifeboats that the officers shot them, and their bodies fell into the ocean.

"It was 11:30 when the collision occurred, and 1:55 o'clock when the ship went down," he said. "Major Archibald Butt stood with John Jacob Astor as the water rolled over the *Titanic*.

Into the Darkness

"I saw Colonel Astor, Major Butt and Captain Smith standing together about 11:30 o'clock. There was absolutely no excitement among them. Captain Smith said there was no danger.

"The starboard side of the *Titanic* struck the big berg and the ice was piled up on the deck. None of us had the slightest realization that the ship had received its death wound.

"Mrs. [Isidor] Straus showed most admirable heroism. She refused in a very determined manner to leave her husband, although she was twice entreated to get into the boats. Straus declined with great force to get in the boat while any women were left.

"I wish you would say for me that Colonel Astor, Major Butt, Captain Smith and every man in the cabins acted the part of a hero in that awful night," Dodge said.

"As the excitement began, I saw an officer of the *Titanic* shoot down two steerage passengers who were endeavoring to rush the lifeboats. I have learned since that twelve of the steerage passengers were shot altogether, one officer shooting down six. The first-cabin men and women behaved with great heroism."

One of the stewards of the *Titanic*, with whom Mrs. and Mrs. Dodge had crossed the Atlantic before on the *Olympic*, knew them well. He recognized Dodge as the thirteenth boat was being filled. The thirteenth boat was filled on one side with children, fully 20 or 30 of them, and a few women. All in the boat were panic-stricken and screaming. The steward had been ordered to take charge of the thirteenth, and, seizing Dodge, pushed him into the boat, exclaiming that he needed his help in caring for his helpless charges.

Dodge said that when the boats were drawing away from the ship they could hear the orchestra playing "Lead, Kindly Light," and rockets were going up from the *Titanic* in the wonderfully clear night. "We could see from the distance that two boats were being made ready to be lowered. The panic was in the steerage, and it was that portion of the ship that the shooting was made necessary.

"I will never forget," Mrs. Dodge said, "the awful scene of the great steamer as we drew away. From the upper rails, heroic husbands and fathers were waving and throwing kisses to their womenfolk in the receding lifeboats."

Colonel Archibald Gracie

Colonel Archibald Gracie, the last man saved, went down with the vessel but was picked up. Colonel Gracie told a remarkable story of personal hardship and denied emphatically the reports that there had been any panic on board. He praised in the highest terms the behavior of both the passengers and crew and paid a high tribute to the heroism of the women passengers.

"Mrs. Isidor Straus," he said, "went to her death because she would not desert her husband. Although he pleaded with her to take her place in the boat she steadfastly refused, and when the ship settled at the head the two were engulfed in the wave that swept her."

Colonel Gracie told of how he was driven to the topmost deck when the ship settled and was the sole survivor after the wave that swept her just before her final plunge had passed.

"I jumped with the wave," he said, "just as I often have jumped with the breakers at the seashore. By great good fortune I managed to grasp the brass railing on the deck above and I hung on by might and main. When the ship plunged down I was forced to let go and I was swirled around and around for what seemed to be an interminable time. Eventually I came to the surface, to find the sea a mass of tangled wreckage.

"Luckily I was unhurt, and casting about, managed to seize a wooden grating floating nearby. When I had recovered my breath, I discovered a larger canvas and cork life raft, which had floated up. A man, whose name I did not learn, was struggling toward it from some wreckage, to which he had clung. I cast off and helped him to get onto the raft and we then began the work of rescuing those who had jumped into the sea and were floundering in the water.

"When dawn broke there were thirty of us on the raft, standing knee deep in the icy water and afraid to move lest the creaky craft be overturned. Several unfortunates, benumbed and half dead, besought us to save them and one or two made an effort to reach us, but we had to warn them away. Had we made any effort to save them, we all might have perished.

"The hours that elapsed before we were picked up by the *Carpathia* were the longest and most terrible that I ever spent. Practically without any sensation of feeling, because of the icy water, we were almost dropping from fatigue. We were afraid to turn around to look to see whether we were seen by passing craft, and when someone who was facing astern passed the word that something that looked like a steamer was coming up, one of the men became hysterical under the strain. The rest of us, too, were nearing the breaking point."

Col. Gracie denied with emphasis that any men were fired upon and declared that only once was a revolver discharged.

"This was for the purpose of intimidating some steerage passengers," he said, "who had tumbled into a boat before it was prepared for launching. This shot was fired in the air, and when the foreigners were told the next would be directed at them, they promptly returned to the deck. There was no confusion and no panic."

"Before I retired," said Colonel Gracie, "I had a long chat with Charles H. Hays, president of the Grand Trunk Railroad. One of the last things Mr. Hays said was this: 'The White Star, the Cunard and the Hamburg-American lines are devoting their attention and ingenuity in vying with them to obtain supremacy in luxurious ships and in making speed records. The time will soon come when this will be checked by some appalling disaster.' Poor fellow; a few hours later, he was dead."

"The conduct of Colonel John Jacob Astor was deserving of the highest praise," declared Colonel Gracie. "The millionaire New Yorker," he said, "devoted all his energies to saving his young bride, Miss Force of New York, who was in delicate health. Colonel Astor helped us in our efforts to get her in the boat," said Colonel Gracie. "I lifted her into the boat and as she took her place. Colonel Astor requested permission of the second officer to go with her for her own protection.

"'No, sir,' replied the officer, 'Not a man shall go on a boat until the women are all off.' Colonel

Into the Darkness

Astor then inquired the number of the boat, which was being lowered away and turned to the work of clearing the other boats and in reassuring the frightened and nervous women.

"By this time the ship began to list frightfully to port. This became so dangerous that the second officer ordered everyone to rush to starboard. This we did and we found the crew trying to get a boat off in that quarter. Here I saw the last of John B. Thayer, second vice president of the Pennsylvania Railroad, and George B. Widener, a capitalist of Philadelphia."

Colonel Gracie said that despite the warnings of icebergs, no slowing down of speed was ordered by the commander of the *Titanic*. There were other warnings, too, he said. "In the 24 hours' run ending the 14th," he said, "the ship's run was 546 miles, and we were told that the next 24 hours would see even a better record posted. No diminution of speed was indicated in the run and the engines kept up their steady running.

"When Sunday evening came, we all noticed the increased cold, which gave plain warning that the ship was in close proximity to icebergs or ice fields. The officers, I am credibly informed, had been advised by wireless from other ships of the presence of icebergs and dangerous floes in that vicinity. The sea was as smooth as glass, and the weather clear, so that it seems that there was no occasion for fear.

"When the vessel struck," Colonel Gracie continued, "the passengers were so little alarmed that they joked over the matter. The few that were on deck early had taken their time to dress properly and there was not the slightest indication of panic. Some of the fragments of ice had fallen on the deck and these were picked up and passed around by some of the facetious ones who offered them as mementoes of the occasion. On the port side, a glance over the side failed to show any evidence of damage and the vessel seemed to be on an even keel. James Clinch Smith and I, however, soon found the vessel was listing heavily. A few minutes later, the officers ordered men and women to don life preservers."

One of the last women seen by Colonel Gracie, he said, was Miss Evans of New York, who virtually refused to be rescued, because, according to the army officer, "she had been told by a fortune teller in London that she would meet her death on the water."

Chapter 6 — Scenes of Desperation and Despair

Standing at the rail of the main deck of the ill-fated *Titanic*, Arthur Ryerson, of Haverford, Pa., waved encouragement to his wife as the lifeboat in which she and her three children—John, Emily and Susan—had been placed with his assistance glided away from the doomed ship. A few minutes later, after the lifeboat with his loved ones had passed beyond the range of his vision, Mr. Ryerson met death in the icy water into which the crushed ship plunged.

It is now known that Mr. Ryerson might have found a place in one of the first lifeboats to be lowered, but made no effort to leave the ship's deck after assuring himself that his wife and children would be saved.

Into the Darkness

It was not until the *Carpathia* reached her dock that relatives who were on hand to meet the survivors of the Ryerson family knew that little "Jack" (John) Ryerson was among the rescued. Day by day since the first tidings of the accident to the *Titanic* were published, "Jack" had been placed among the missing.

Perhaps of all those who came up from the *Carpathia* with the impress of the tragedy upon them, the homecoming of Mrs. Ryerson was peculiarly sad.

While motoring with J. Lewis Hoffman, of Radnor, Pa., on the Main Line, on Monday a week before, Arthur L. Ryerson, her son, was killed. His parents abandoned their plans for a summer pleasure trip through Europe and took passage on the first homebound ship, which happened to be the *Titanic*, to attend the funeral of their son. And now upon one tragedy a second presses.

Upon leaving the *Carpathia*, Mrs. Ryerson, almost too exhausted and weak to tell of her experiences, was taken in a taxicab to the Hotel Belmont. With her were her son "Jack" and her two daughters, Emily and Susan Ryerson.

The young women were hysterical with grief as they walked up from the dock, and the little lad who had witnessed such sights of horror and tragedy, clung to his mother's hand, wide eyed and sorrowful.

Mrs. Ryerson said that she and her husband were asleep in their staterooms, as were their children, when the terrible grating crash came and the ship foundered. The women threw kimonos over their night gowns and rushed barefooted to the deck. Master Ryerson's nurse caught up a few articles of the little boy's clothing and almost as soon as the party reached the deck they were numbered off into boats and lowered into the sea.

Mrs. John M. Brown

Mrs. John M. Brown, of Boston, described her experience on the *Titanic* as the "most harrowing and terrible that any living soul could undergo."

"Oh, it was heart-rending to see those brave men die," Mrs. Brown said, half-sobbingly, after she had left the pier in a taxicab brought by her husband.

Mr. Brown, for his part, said the days of agony which he had experienced, when the lists of *Titanic* survivors were altered, diminished and published incomplete, leaving him indecisive as to his wife's fate, was almost on a par what she had undergone.

In contradiction to several other statements, Mrs. Brown declared that she saw no signs of panic or disorder on the *Titanic* and did not know until later that there had been shooting on board the vessel.

"I was in my berth when the crash came," Mrs. Brown said, "and after the first shock when I knew instinctively that the vessel was sinking, I was comparatively calm.

"I had hardly reached deck when an officer called to me to enter a lifeboat. I did so, and saw the huge liner split in half, with a pang almost as keen as if I had seen somebody die."

Mrs. Brown said that John B. Thayer, Jr., after jumping from the deck of the liner, clad only in pajamas, swam through cakes of floating ice to a broken raft. He was picked up by the boat of which Mrs. Brown was an occupant.

Into the Darkness

Mrs. Brown said that it was about two hours after the *Titanic* sank that their boat came within sight of an object bobbing up and down in the cakes of ice, about fifty yards away. Nearing, they made out the form of a boy clinging with one leg and both arms wrapped around the piece of wreckage. Young Thayer uttered feeble cries as they pulled alongside.

The lad was pulled into the already crowded lifeboat exhausted. With a weak, faint smile, Mrs. Brown said, the lad collapsed.

Women, who were not rowing or assisting in maneuvering the boat, by vigorous rubbing, soon brought Thayer to consciousness and shared part of their scanty attire to keep him from dying from exposure. In the meantime, the boat bobbed about on the waves like a top, frequently striking cakes of ice.

Mrs. Brown said for several hours more they battled with the sea before help arrived.

"It was a blessed sight when all saw the *Carpathia* heading in our din," she declared. "We had hopes that a ship would come to our rescue and all on board prayed for safe deliverance.

"No one can realize our feeling of gratitude when the *Carpathia* emerged into sight. With increased energy, the men, aided by the women, pulled on the oars. We were soon taken aboard. Young Thayer was hurried into the hospital on board the boat and was given stimulants and revived.

"Three survivors died soon after; they were buried at sea. Mrs. Brown said that Mrs. John Jacob Astor, the wife of Colonel John Jacob Astor, who proved himself a hero, was also an occupant of her boat.

Into the Darkness

"Mrs. Astor was frantic when she learned that her husband had gone with the *Titanic*, but between sobs said he died a hero," Mrs. Brown said.

"The colonel kissed her and pushing his bride to the side of the ship, told her to hurry to the lifeboats awaiting below.

"Mrs. Astor refused to listen to her husband's entreaties until he assured her that he would follow on the next boat, although all the time he knew that he would sink."

"The following horrors have never left me, day or night," Mrs. Brown continued.

"I saw dead bodies of brave men float past the lifeboats. I heard the death cries of women and saw the terrible desolation of the wreck by dawn."

In the boat with Mrs. Brown were her two sisters, Mrs. Robert Cornell, wife of Judge Robert Cornell, and Mrs. S.P. Appleton.

They followed each other down the long, roughly constructed rope ladder, a distance of more than fifty feet, into the tenth lifeboat. All were thinly clad. They had retired for the night and were tumbled from their berths when the crash came.

Photograph of an iceberg in the vicinity of the RMS *Titanic's* sinking taken on 15 April 1912.

Mrs. Churchill Candee

"The men were the heroes," said Mrs. Churchill Candee, of Washington, one of the survivors, "and among the bravest and most heroic, as I recall, were Mr. Widener, Mr. Thayer and Colonel Astor. They thought only of the saving of the women and went down with the *Titanic*, martyrs to their manhood.

"I saw Mr. and Mrs. Isidor Straus on the deck of the *Titanic* as I was lowered into one of the lifeboats. Mrs. Straus refused to leave the ship unless her husband could accompany her. They were on the top deck, and I heard her say she would not leave her husband. She went down with him as she had lived and traveled with him. Life without him did not concern her, seemingly. 'I've always stayed with my husband, so why should I leave him now? I'll die with him,' I heard her say."

"Captain Smith, I think, sacrificed safety in a treacherous ice field for speed. He was trying to make 570 miles for the day, I heard. The captain, who had stood waist deep on the deck of the *Titanic* as she sank, jumped as the ship went down, but he was drowned. All of the men had bravely faced their doom for the women and children.

"The ship settled slowly, the lights going out deck after deck as the water reached them. The final plunge, however, was sudden and accompanied by explosions, the effect of which was a horrible sight. Victims standing on the upper deck toward the stern were hurled into the air and fell into the treacherous ice-covered sea. Some were rescued, but most of them perished. I cannot help recalling again that Mr. Widener and Mr. Thayer and Colonel Astor died manfully.

"The ice pack, which we encountered," explained Mrs. Candee, "was fifty-six miles long, I have since heard. When we collided with the mountainous mass, it was nearly midnight Sunday. There were two distinct shocks, each shaking the ship violently, but fear did not spread among the passengers immediately. They seemed not to realize what had happened, but the captain and other officers did not endeavor to minimize the danger.

"The first thing I recall was one of the crew appearing with pieces of ice in his hands. He said he had gathered them from the bow of the boat. Some of the passengers were inclined to believe he was joking. But soon the situation dawned on all of us. The lifeboats were ordered lowered and manned and the word went around that women and children were to be taken off first. The men stood back as we descended to the frail craft or assisted us to disembark."

Chapter 7 — Astonishing Rescues and Emotional Final Moments

Lola and Momon, the little waifs of the *Titanic* disaster, snatched from the sea and kept for a month in a big, strange land, were clasped in the arms of their mother Mme. Marcelle Navratil, who arrived in New York, on May 16, from France on the White Star liner *Oceanic*.

Hurrying down the gangplank, after kindly customs officials had facilitated her landing, Mme. Navratil, who was an Italian, 24 years old, of remarkable beauty, rushed to Miss Margaret Hays, the rescuer of the two little boys, who, with her father, was waiting on the pier. They took her in a cab to the Children's Society rooms, and there she was reunited with her children.

The little boys, four and two years old, were thrust into one of the last of the lifeboats to leave the sinking *Titanic* by an excited Frenchmen, who asked that they be cared for. A steward told him he could not enter the boat and he said he did not want to, but must save his boys.

Arriving in New York on the *Carpathia*, Miss Hays at first could learn nothing of the children's identity, and she planned to care for them. Then another chapter of the weird story developed. The Frenchman's body was recovered and taken to Halifax, where it was found that he was booked on the passenger list under the name of "Hoffman."

Cable messages to France brought the information that Mme. Narvatil's husband, from whom she was separated, had kidnapped her children and said he was going to America. He often used the name "Hoffman." Photographs of the boys were sent to

Mme. Navratil in France, and she identified them as her children.

Separating fact from fiction

A number of interesting facts stand out from the chaotic accounts of the tragedy. These are some of the most salient:

- The death list was increased rather than decreased. Six persons died after being rescued.
- The list of prominent persons lost stood as at first reported.
- Practically every woman and child, with the exception of those women who refused to leave their husbands, were saved. Among the last was Mrs. Isidor Straus.
- The survivors in the lifeboats saw the lights on the stricken vessel glimmer to the last, heard her band playing and saw the doomed

hundreds on her deck and heard their groans and cries when the vessel sank.

Accounts vary as to the extent of the disorder on board.

Not only was the *Titanic* tearing through the April night to her doom with every ounce of steam crowded on, but she was under orders from the general officers of the line to make all the speed of which she was capable. This was the statement made by J.H. Moody, a quartermaster of the vessel and helmsman on the night of the disaster. He said the ship was making 21 knots an hour, and the officers were striving to live up to the orders to smash the records.

"It was close to midnight," said Moody, "and I was on the bridge with the second officer, who was in command. Suddenly, he shouted 'Port your helm!' I did so, but it was too late. We struck the submerged portion of the berg."

Of the many accounts given by the passengers, most of them agreed that the shock when the *Titanic* struck the iceberg, although ripping her great sides like a giant can opener, did not greatly jar the entire vessel, for the blow was a glancing one along her side. The accounts also agree substantially that when the passengers were taken off on the lifeboats, there was no serious panic and that many wished to remain on board the *Titanic*, believing her to be unsinkable.

The most distressing stories are those giving the experiences of the passengers in lifeboats. These tell not only of their own suffering, but give the harrowing details of how they saw the great hulk of the *Titanic* stand on end, stern uppermost for many minutes before plunging to the bottom. As this spectacle was witnessed by the groups of survivors in the boats, they plainly saw many of those whom they had just left behind leaping from the decks into the water.

Henry Stengel's remarkable story

A statement from Henry E. Stengel outlined the horrors of the wreck and the nerve-racking voyage on the rescue ship *Carpathia*. Mr. Stengel spoke in stern terms of the recklessness that made the accident so appalling. Although it was near to midnight when he and his wife reached Newark, there were a hundred friends waiting to receive them, all of whom hung breathlessly on the recital of the perils which the two escaped.

Mr. Stengel and his wife had one of the most remarkable reunions of any persons on the ship. The two did not escape in the same boat—Mrs. Stengel being in the first launched, while her husband was in the very last boat from the starboard side. Mrs. Stengel looked many years older than when she left the other side a few weeks ago, and was even more emphatic than her husband in criticism of the shortcomings of the White Star officials.

"There was absolutely no water in our boat. We would have died of thirst if rescue had not been near at hand," she said. "I understand it was that way in all the other lifeboats, few of which even had lanterns. I have heard that a couple of them were provided with bread at the last moment, but our boat was absolutely without any food."

Mrs. Stengel was worn by the constant strain that had been pressing upon her in the last five days.

"This has been such a terrible worry that I feel as though I could never sleep again," she said. "Oh, it was horrible, horrible. Sometimes I think that I would have been better dead than to have so much to remember. You see when the crash first came no one realized the awful seriousness of the situation. It was a loud, grinding crash and it shook the boat like a leaf, but we had all become so filled with the idea that the *Titanic* was a creation greater than the seas that no one was terror-stricken. Some of the women screamed and children cried, but they told us it was all right and that nothing serious could happen.

"I was just preparing for sleep when the crash came, and throwing on some clothes, I rushed on deck with my husband. In a short time we were told that the women would be sent in the boats. I did not want to leave my husband, but he laughed and told me that the boating was only temporary. There was very little confusion when we put off and the men in the first and second cabins were absolutely calm. Mr. Stengel kissed me and told me not to worry, that he would come in a later boat, unless it was decided to bring us back on the ship.

"For some reason no attention was paid to the men who were put in our boat. One of them was an undersized Chinaman and the other was an Oriental of some kind. When the lifeboat struck the water, they crawled up in the bottom and began to moan and cry. They refused to take their places at the oars and first class women passengers had to man many of the row-locks. Still none of us thought that the great *Titanic* would sink. We rowed two hundred yards away, as they had told us, watching the great ship. Then the lights began to go out and then came a terrible crash like dynamite."

Mrs. Stengel continued: "I heard a woman in the bow scream and then came three more terrific explosions. The boat gave a sudden lurch and then we saw the men jumping from the decks. Some of us prayed and I heard women curse, but the most terrible thing was the conduct of the Chinaman and the Oriental. They threw themselves about the boat in absolute fits and almost upset the boat. They were a menace during the whole night and in the morning when the light began to come in the east, and when the women were exhausted from trying to man the oars, the two of them found some cigarettes and lay in the bottom of the boat and smoked while we tried to work the oars."

There was no survivor better qualified to tell of the last incidents aboard the vessel than Mr. Stengel. He was one of the last three men to leave the boat. He was a man of scientific turn-of-mind and held some valuable data concerning the wreck.

"As my wife has told you, there was but little disorder on board after the crash," he said. "I realized the seriousness of the situation immediately, because I saw Captain Smith come out of the cabin. He was closely followed by Mr. and Mrs. George Widener, of Philadelphia.

"'What is the outlook?' I heard Mr. Widener inquire. 'It is extremely serious, gentlemen,' he said. 'Please keep cool and do what you can to help us.'"

Mr. Stengel continued. "Deck stewards rushed through the corridors rapping frantically on the doors of the occupied cabins. All were told that the danger was imminent. Some heeded and grasping the first clothing they could find, they rushed on deck. Others refused to come out. They would not believe there was danger.

"On deck the boat crews were all at their posts. The big lifeboats had been shoved around ready to be put over the side. Women and children were picked up bodily and thrown into them. The rule of the sea, women and children first, was being enforced.

"One after the other the boats went over the side. Then a cry was set up: 'There are no more boats!' was the shout. Consternation seized upon all that remained. They had believed there would be room for all. Uncontrollable terror seized many. They fought for the life belts. Some frantically tried to tear loose deck fittings hoping to make small rafts that would sustain them until help would come. But everything was bolted fast. Then, fearful that they would be dragged to death in the swirling suction that would follow, the men began to leap into the ice filled ocean.

"It was his face, more than anything else, which made me fearful," continued Mr. Stengel. "He looked like an old, old man. I heard him give instructions to his officers, and they took their stations at the boats. I did not see anyone shot during the whole wreck. They fired three shots in the air to show the steerage men that the guns were loaded, but I was on the boat almost to the last, and I didn't see anyone shot. The boat which saved me was not a regular lifeboat, but a light emergency boat. There was a great rush for it. By the time it was launched, the first fear had subsided. It was the last to be lowered from the starboard side.

"The *Titanic* seemed to be floating safely, and a lot of people preferred it to the flimsy looking rowboats. A deckhand told me that there was a vacant place in it. There I found Sir Cosmo Duff-Gordon, Lady Duff- Gordon and their maid, Miss Francatelli. Just as the boat was being lowered, Mr. A.L. Solomon jumped in. We had gone but a little way from the ship when the first boiler explosion came. It was followed in quick succession by three others, at intervals of about one second apart."

Into the Darkness

In the boat that harbored Mr. Stengel were three stokers and two members of the steerage. Mr. Stengel told graphically of the last plunges of the ship and its final sinking. He declared that there was a little eddy and no whirlpool when it sank. Many of the men on the *Titanic* jumped into sea before the decks were awash. In telling of the long night on the sea, Mr. Stengel gave great credit to a member of the crew who had taken three green lanterns on board just as the small lifeboat was manned.

He said that it was the only beacon which the other lifeboats had for guidance, and said that without it many more would surely have been lost.

Mrs. Stengel spoke particularly of the calmness of the night.

"When the sun rose there was not a ripple on the water," she said. "It was as calm as a little lake in Connecticut. Words cannot express the wonderful terrible beauty of it all—but of course, I couldn't appreciate it, because I thought my husband had gone down in the sea.

"The shout of 'land' ever uttered by an explorer was not half so joyful as the shout of 'ship!' which went up when the *Carpathia* appeared on the horizon that morning," she said. "The first dim lights, which appeared were eagerly watched and when it was really identified as a ship, men and women broke down and wept."

The reunion of Mr. and Mrs. Stengel was on the *Carpathia*. Each was mourning the other as lost for more than an hour after they had been on the vessel, when they met on the promenade deck. Their separation and subsequent reunion was generally considered one of the most remarkable in the history of the wreck.

Into the Darkness

Passengers describe intense final moments

They jumped in groups, seemingly to an agreed signal, according to the stories of the survivors. Some who jumped were saved, coming up near lifeboats and being dragged into them by the occupants.

Slowly, steadily and majestically the liner sank. One deck after the other was submerged. Whether the boilers exploded is a question. Robert W. Daniel, a Philadelphia banker, says that when the icy water poured into the boiler room, two separate explosions followed that tore the interior out of the liner. Others say they did not hear any explosions.

The plight of the survivors in the boats was pitiful in the extreme. Few of the women or children had sufficient clothing, and they shivered in the bitter cold blasts that came from the great field of ice which surrounded them. The bergs and cakes of drift ice crashed and thundered, bringing stark terror to the helpless victims.

Daybreak found the little flotilla bobbing and tossing on the surface of the ocean. It was not known whether help was coming. Panic seized some of the occupants; some of the women tried to jump into the water, and had to be forcibly restrained. The babies, little tots, just old enough to realize their position, found themselves heroes. They set an example, which moved their elders to tears as they told of it. Some tried to comfort their stricken parents.

Finally, off in the distant horizon, a sailor in the leading boat, discerned smoke. "We are saved," went up the cry, and the rescue came just in time, for before the *Carpathia* had taken aboard the occupants of the last frail craft, the waves were increasing in height, kicked up by the wind that had increased with the rising of the sun.

All were tenderly cared for on the Cunard liner. The regular passengers willingly gave up their cabins to their unfortunate refugees, medical aid was forthcoming, and nothing left undone that could relieve the distress.

Chapter 8 — Screams Echo across a Sea of Glass

Mrs. May Futrelle, whose husband, Jacques Futrelle, went down with the ship, was met in New York by her daughter, Miss Virginia Futrelle.

The young Miss Futrelle had been told that her father had been picked up by another steamer. Mrs. Charles Copeland, of Boston, a sister of Mr. Futrelle, who also met Mrs. Futrelle, was under the same impression.

"I am so happy that father is safe, too," declared Miss Futrelle, as her mother embraced her in her arms. It was some time before Mrs. Futrelle could compose herself.

"Where is Jack?" Mrs. Copeland asked.

Into the Darkness

Mrs. Futrelle, afraid to let her daughter know the truth, said: "Oh, he is on another ship."

Mrs. Copeland soon guessed the truth and became hysterical. Then the daughter broke down.

"Jack died like a hero," Mrs. Futrelle said, when the party became composed. "He was in the smoking-room when the crash came—the noise of the smash was terrific—and I was going to bed. I was hurled from my feet by the impact. I hardly found myself when Jack came rushing into the stateroom.

"The boat is going down, get dressed at once!" he shouted. "When we reached the deck everything was in the wildest confusion. The screams of women and the shrill orders of the officers were drowned intermittently by the tremendous vibrations of the *Titanic*'s bass foghorn.

Into the Darkness

"The behavior of the men was magnificent. They stood back without murmuring and urged the women and children into the lifeboats. A few cowards tried to scramble into the boats, but they were quickly thrown back by the others. Let me say now that the only men who were saved were those who sneaked into the lifeboats or were picked up after the *Titanic* sank.

"I did not want to leave Jack, but he assured me that there were boats enough for all and that he would be rescued later.

"'Hurry up, May, you're keeping the others waiting,' were his last words, as he lifted me into a lifeboat and kissed me good-bye. I was in one of the last lifeboats to leave the ship. We had not put out many minutes when the *Titanic* disappeared. I almost thought, as I saw her sink beneath the water, that I could see Jack, standing where I had left him and waving at me."

Mrs. Futrelle said she saw the parting of Colonel John Jacob Astor and his young bride. Mrs. Astor was frantic. Her husband had to jump into the lifeboat four times and tell her that he would be rescued later. After the fourth time, Mrs. Futrelle said, he jumped back on the deck of the sinking ship and the lifeboat bearing his bride made off.

George D. Widener

George D. Widener and his son, Harry Elkins Widener, lost in the wreck of the *Titanic*, died the death of heroes. They stood back that the weaker might have a chance of being saved.

Mrs. Widener, one of the last women to leave the ship, fought to die with her husband and her son. She would have succeeded probably had not sailors literally torn her from her husband and forced her on to a life-raft.

As she descended the ladder at the ship's side, compelled to leave despite her frantic, despairing pleas, she called to Mr. Widener and to her son pitifully.

"Oh, my God!" she cried. "Good-bye! George! Harry! Good-bye! Good-bye! Oh, God! This is awful!" And that was the last she saw of her husband and of her son, who waved a brave farewell as she disappeared down the ladder.

Mr. Widener and his son Harry helped the women and the children to make their escape, but always stood back themselves when a boat or raft was launched. As soon as the vessel had struck the iceberg Mr. and Mrs. Widener had sought out Captain Smith.

"What is the outlook?" Mr. Widener was heard to inquire.

"It is extremely serious," was the quick reply. "Please keep cool and do what you can to help us." And this is what Mr. Widener did.

James B. McGough

Also among the rescued was James B. McGough, who gave the following account:

"When the crash came, I ran to the porthole. I saw the ice pressed close against the side of the ship. Chunks of it were ground off, and they fell into the window. I happened to glance at my watch, and it showed me exactly the hour.

"I knew that something was seriously wrong and hastily got into my clothes. I took time, also, to get my watch and money. In the meantime, J.D. Flynn, who occupied the room with me, had run over to Calderhead's stateroom and had awakened him. When I had dressed I ran outside.

"I saw the iceberg. The boat deck stood about ninety feet out of the water and the berg towered above us for at least fifty feet. I judge the berg stood between 140 and 150 feet out of the water.

"Many of the women on board, I am sure, did not leave their staterooms at once," he said. "They stayed there, at least for a time. I believe that many of them did not awaken to their danger until near the last.

"One statement I want to correct, the lights did not go out, at least not while I was on board. When I ran to the deck I heard Captain Smith order that the air chambers be examined. An effort was made to work the doors closing the compartments, but to no avail.

When the ship ran upon the iceberg, the sharp-pointed berg cut through both thicknesses of the bottom and left it in such a position that it filled rapidly."

McGough continued: "I remember that it was a beautiful night. There was no wind and the sea was calm. But for this, it is certain that when the boats were launched, most all of us would have perished in the ice-covered sea. At first, the captain ordered the hatches over the steerage fastened down. This was to prevent the hysterical passengers in that part of the ship rushing to the deck and increasing the panic. Before we left, however, those passengers were released.

"Two sailors were put into each of the boats. When the boats were lowered the women hung back. They feared to go down the long, steep ladder to the water. Seeing them hesitate, I cried: 'Someone has to be first,' and started down the ladder.

"I had hardly started before I regretted I had not waited on deck. But I feel if I had not led the way, the women would not have started and the death list would have been much larger. Flynn and Calderhead led the way into other boats.

"It was only a short time before the boat was filled. We had fifty-five in our boat, nearly all of them women. We had entered the craft so hastily that we did not take time to get a light," said McGough.

"For a time we bobbed about on the ocean. Then we started to row slowly away. I shall never forget the screams that flowed over the ocean toward us from the sinking ship. At the end there was a mad rush and scramble.

"It was fearfully hard on the women. Few of them were completely dressed. Some wore only their night gowns, with some light wrapper or kimono over them. The air was pitilessly cold.

"There were so few men in the boat the women had to row. This was good for some of them, as it kept their blood in circulation, but even then it was the most severe experience for them imaginable. Some of them were half-crazed with grief or terror. Several became ill from the exposure.

"I saw Mr. Widener just before I left, and afterward, while we were rowing away from the vessel I had a good glimpse of him. He appeared as calm and collected as though he were taking a walk on Broad Street. When the rush for the boats began, he and his son Harry, stood back.

"At the end, sailors had to tear Mrs. Widener from him, and she went down the ladder, calling to him pitifully. The ship went down at 2:20 o'clock exactly. The front end went down gradually. We saw no men shot, but just before the finish, we heard several shots.

"I was told that Captain Smith or one of the officers shot himself on the bridge just before the *Titanic* went under. I heard also that several men had been killed as they made a final rush for the boats, trying to cut off the women and children."

McGough continued: "While we were floating around the sailors set off some redfire, which illuminated the ocean for miles around. This was a signal of distress. Unfortunately, there was no one near enough to answer in time.

Into the Darkness

"John B. Thayer, Jr., was saved after he had gone down with the ship. Just as the vessel took the plunge he leaped over the side. He struck out for a life raft and reached it. There he clung for several hours until, half-frozen, he was taken into one of the boats which was a trifle less crowded than the others.

"For six hours we bobbed around in the ocean. We rowed over to a boat that was provided with a light, and tied the two small craft together. Finally daylight came, and the sun rose in a clear sky. There we were, a little fleet, alone in the limitless ocean, with the ice cakes tossing about on all sides.

"It was after 8 o'clock in the morning when we saw the masts of a steamship coming up over the horizon. It was the most blessed sight our eyes ever saw. It meant an end to the physical suffering, a relief to the strain under which we had been laboring. Many broke down when they saw it.

"The ship, of course, was the *Carpathia*. While it was hurrying toward us, the crew and passengers had made the most generous preparations for us. When they took us on board they had blankets, clothing, food and warm liquids all ready. Their physicians were ready to care for the sick. The passengers gave up their warm beds to us.

"During the time we were in the water we bumped frequently into the bodies that floated about us. A great many of the men jumped into the water before the boat sank, and they were the bodies that we struck."

Chapter 9 — Life and Death Decisions

D.H. Bishop, a rich lumber man of Dowagiac, Mich., who with his wife, was returning from a bridal trip to Egypt, is the last person known to have seen George D. Widener alive. Mr. Bishop said:

"My wife and I had just retired when we heard the jar and felt a decided tilt of the ship. I got up and started to investigate, but soon became reassured and went back to bed. A few minutes later we heard calls to put on life belts.

"My wife felt very alarmed and kneeled to pray. She said she knew we would be lost, though at that time there was no reason to think so, and she remarked: 'What is the use bothering with jewelry if we are going to die?' Accordingly, she left in her stateroom jewelry worth about $11,000, but strangely enough insisted upon me running back and getting her muff.

"As we came up the stairway we met Captain Smith and Colonel John Jacob Astor talking hurriedly. What they said I do not know. When we got on deck there were not more than fifty people there and no one seemed excited and no one appeared to want to get into the lifeboats, though urged to do so. Mrs. Bishop and I were literally lifted into the first lifeboat.

"At that time I observed Mr. and Mrs. Widener, and I saw the former leave his wife as she was getting into the lifeboat and, accompanied by his son, go toward the stairway. I did not see them again, as our lifeboat with only twenty-eight persons in it and only half-manned, was lowered over the side at that moment. An instant later, there was an apparent rush for the lifeboats and as we rowed away, they came over the side with great rapidity.

"Before we were a hundred yards away, men were jumping overboard, and when we were a mile away, the ship went down with cries from the men and women aboard that were heart-rending.

"There is nothing to say concerning the blame, except that I do know that icebergs were known to be in our vicinity and that it was the subject of much talk that the *Titanic* was out for a record. Captain Smith was dining with J. Bruce Ismay, managing director of the White Star Line, and of course, was not on the bridge. It was rumored on the *Carpathia* that Captain Smith tried to save himself in a lifeboat at the last minute, but of this, I know nothing."

Survivors tell of perilous escapes

Major Arthur Puechen, a wealthy resident of Toronto, Canada, was the last man on the *Titanic* to say goodbye to Charles M. Hays, president of the Grand Trunk Pacific Railway, who lost his life.

After assisting members of the crew in filling up the first five boats, Major Puechen, an experienced yachtsman, was assigned by the second mate to take charge of boat No. 6. Major Puechen said he declined to accept such a post, not desiring to have any preference over any of his fellow passengers.

Captain Smith, wishing an experienced boatsman on boat No. 6, directed the second officer to give the Major a written order to take charge of it. Just as the Major was about to leave in the lifeboat, his old friend, Charles M. Hays, of the Grand Trunk, came up and said goodbye. Mr. Hays had no idea, according to Major Puechen, that the ship would sink as soon as it did, but believed that help would be at hand sufficient to care for all before the vessel went down.

Mr. Hays remarked to the Major that the ship could not possibly sink within eight hours, and that long before then everybody would be taken off safely. Mr. Hays expressed no fear that he would be lost by remaining on board the ship.

Peter D. Daly, of New York, jumped from the deck of the *Titanic* after it was announced that there were only boats enough for the women and children. As he saw the ship settling gradually he swam away with all his might to prevent being carried down with the suction of the sinking liner.

"For six hours I beat the water with hands and feet to keep warm," he said. "Then I was picked up by one of the *Carpathia*'s boats, which was cruising around looking for survivors. I was numb from the cold, after a fight which I can scarcely bear to discuss.

"Even after I recovered from the chill and shock, I was practically prostrated by the nervous strain, and every mention of the disaster sends a shiver through me.

"There was no violent impact when the vessel collided with the ice," Daly said. "I rushed to the deck from my cabin, got a life preserver and, when things began to look serious, threw myself into the water. The boat had already begun to settle."

A huge cake of ice was the means of aiding Emile Portaluppi, of Aricgabo, Italy, in escaping death when the *Titanic* went down. Portaluppi, a second class passenger, was awakened by the explosion of one of the boilers of the ship. He hurried to the deck, strapped a life preserver around him and leaped into the sea. With the aid of the preserver and by holding to a cake of ice, he managed to keep afloat until one of the lifeboats picked him up. There were 35 people in the boat when he was hauled aboard.

Mrs. Fred R. Kenyon, of Southington, Conn., was one of the *Titanic*'s survivors. Her husband went down with the vessel rather than take the place of a woman in a boat. Mrs. Kenyon said that when the call was given for the women to take places near the boat davits, in readiness to be placed in the boats as they were swung off, Mr. Kenyon was by her side. When it came her turn to enter the boat, Mr. Kenyon helped his wife to a place and kissed her goodbye. Mrs. Kenyon said she asked him to come with her, and he replied: "I would not with all those women and children waiting to get off."

In an instant, Mr. Kenyon had stepped back and other women took their places and the boat swung clear and dropped to the water. In the boat, Mrs. Kenyon said there were one sailor and three men who had been ordered in because they said they could row.

Mrs. Lucien P. Smith, daughter of Representative James P. Hughes, of West Virginia, a bride of about eight weeks, whose husband was lost in the wreck, gave the details of her experience through her uncle, Dr. J. H. Vincent, of Huntington, West Virginia.

"The women were shoved into the lifeboats," said Dr. Vincent. "The crew did not wait until the lifeboat was filled before they lowered it. As a matter of fact, there were but 26 people in the boat, mostly all women, when an officer gave instructions to lower it. Mr. Smith was standing alongside the boat when it was lowered. There was plenty of room for more people to get into the lifeboats, the capacity being fifty.

Into the Darkness

"Mrs. Smith implored Captain Smith to allow her husband in the boat, but her repeated appeals, however, were ignored," Dr. Vincent said. "This lifeboat was permitted to be lowered with but one sailor in it and he was drunk. His condition was such that he could not row the boat and therefore the women had to do the best they could in rowing about the icy waters.

"As the boat swung out from the side it was evident that the three men knew absolutely nothing about rowing and Mrs. Kenyon said she and another woman seized the oars and helped the sailors to pull clear. Gradually the small boat was worked away from the *Titanic*. The boat had gone quite a distance when suddenly all heard a terrific explosion and in the glare, which followed, they saw the body of a man hurled from the bridge high in the air. Then darkness fell. At 6.30 the boat was picked up by the *Carpathia*."

Into the Darkness

Kate Mullin, of County Longford, Ireland, told of how stewards had tried to keep back the steerage women. She said she saw scores of men and women jump overboard and drown.

Bunar Tonglin, a Swede, was saved in the next to the last boat that left the *Titanic*. Before getting into the boat, he placed two hysterical women in another boat. Then he heard a cry, and, looking up, saw a woman standing on the upper deck. The woman, he said, dropped from her arms her baby, which Tonglin caught, and gave to one of the women he had put in the boat. Then he got into his own boat, which was lowered, and shortly afterwards came the two explosions, and the plunge downward of the *Titanic*. Tonglin declared that he had seen numerous persons leap from the decks of the *Titanic* and drown.

John B. Thayer

Mrs. John B. Thayer, whose husband, the second vice-president of the Pennsylvania Railroad, went down with the *Titanic*, after heroically standing aside to allow his wife's maid to take his place in the lifeboat. Her son, John B. Thayer, Jr., was pulled aboard a lifeboat after being thrown from the giant liner just before she sank.

The son had proven himself in the critical moment. Shortly after the *Titanic* crashed into the iceberg, Mr. Thayer had collected his wife, his son and his wife's maid and gotten them in line for a lifeboat. Realizing that there was not enough room for the men, Mr. Thayer forced his wife and her maid into the boat and then tried to get his son in also.

The lad, however, refused to desert his father. Stepping back, he made room for someone else, said to have been a grown man, and grasping his father's hand, said he "guessed he would stick by dad." Before Mr. Thayer could protest or forcibly place his son in the lifeboat, it had been launched and the opportunity was gone.

A few seconds before the *Titanic* sank, however, Mr. Thayer seemed to grasp the fact that the end was near. Picking up the boy he threw him into the sea. "Swim to a boat my boy," he said.

Young Thayer, taken by surprise, had no chance to object. Before he knew what had happened, he was struggling in the icy waters of the ocean. Striking out, the lad swam to a lifeboat, but was beaten off by some of those aboard, as the boat was already overcrowded.

But the pluck that has made so many Thayers famous as athletes in many branches of sport was deeply implanted in young "Jack" Thayer. Turning from the lifeboat from which he had been beaten off, he swam to another. Once again he was fended away with a long oar. And all this time Mrs. Thayer, safe in another boat, watched her son struggle for life, too overcome with horror to even scream.

A few seconds later the *Titanic* went down. There was a swirling of the waters, though not as much suction as had been expected. To save himself from the tug of the in-draw waters, young Thayer grasped a floating cake of ice. To this he clung until another boat, filled with people of more kindly hearts, came by and pulled him aboard.

In this boat was Miss Brown, a friend of the boy's mother. She took charge of him until they were taken on board the *Carpathia*. Mrs. Thayer had not seen the rescue of her son. She had fainted, it is said, but revived a few moments later and did yeoman service at the oars. Other survivors in her boat spoke in the highest terms of her calm courage, which served to keep up the spirits of the women, half frozen from the bitter cold, insufficiently clad and bereft of their loved ones. Taking an oar, without waiting to be asked, she used every ounce of her strength for long hours before the *Carpathia* arrived, aiding the few sailors aboard to keep the boat's head to the sea and to dodge the myriads of ice cakes.

The exercise, however, served to keep her warm, and when she was lifted to the deck of the *Carpathia* she did not need hospital treatment. Her son, however, was in bad shape when he was rescued. His clothing was frozen to his body and he was exhausted from his battle with the ice-filled sea. Restoratives and hot water bottles in the *Carpathia*'s hospital brought him around in time, however, and the moment he was able to stand on his feet he rushed through the ship, seeking his mother. That

Into the Darkness

was a joyful reunion for both, but particularly for Mrs. Thayer, as she had given her son up for lost.

Speaking for himself of his experience, the young Jack Thayer said, "I was with father. They wanted me to go into a boat, but I wanted to stay with him. Men and women kept calling to me to hurry and jump in a boat, but it wasn't any use. I knew what I was doing. It didn't seem to be anything to be afraid about. Some of the men were laughing. Nobody appeared to be excited. We had struck with a smash and then we seemed to slide off backwards from the big field of ice. It was cold, but we didn't mind that.

"The boats were put off without much fuss. Mother was put into one of the boats. As I said, she wanted me to go with her. But I said I guessed I would stick with dad. After a while I felt the ship tipping toward the front. The next thing I knew, somebody gave me a push and I was in the water. Down, down, down, I went, ever so far. It seemed as if I never would stop. I couldn't breathe. Then I shot up through the water just as fast as I went down. I had just time to take a long, deep breath when a wave went over me."

Thayer continued: "When I came to the surface a second time I swam to a boat. They wouldn't take me in. Then I tried another. Same result. Finally, when I was growing weak, I bumped against something. I found it was an overturned lifeboat. It was a struggle to pull myself upon it, but I did it after a while. My, it was cold! I never suffered so much in my life. All around were the icebergs.

"I could see boats on all sides. I must have shouted, because my throat was all raw and sore, but nobody seemed to notice. I guess they all were shouting, too. Every part of me ached with the cold. I thought I was going to die. It seemed as if I couldn't stand it any longer.

Into the Darkness

"The time was so long and I was so weak. Then I just couldn't feel anything anymore. I knew if I stayed there I would freeze. A boat came by and I swam to it. They took me aboard. The next thing I remember clearly was when the boat from the *Carpathia* came and I was taken into it and wrapped up in the coats of the men. They told me I was more than three hours on that raft and in that open boat. It seemed more like three years to me."

Into the Darkness

Only two of the 18 launched lifeboats rescued people after the ship sank. Lifeboat 4 was close by
and picked up five people, two of whom later died.

Chapter 10 — Last Goodbyes and Touching Reunions

"If anything should happen to me, tell my wife in New York that I've done my best in doing my duty."

This was the last message of Benjamin Guggenheim, of the famous banking family, dictated to a steward only a short while before the banker sank to his death with the *Titanic*.

It was not until several days later that the message was received by Mrs. Guggenheim. It was delivered by James Etches, assistant steward in the first cabin of the *Titanic*, to whom Mr. Guggenheim communicated it. Etches appeared at the St. Regis Hotel and inquired for Mrs. Benjamin Guggenheim. He said that he had a message from Benjamin

Guggenheim, and that it had to be delivered in person. The steward was admitted, but was not permitted to see Mrs. Guggenheim. He insisted that he must see her personally, but finally consented to transmit the message through her brother-in-law.

"We were together almost to the end," said the steward. "I was saved. He went down with the ship. But that isn't what I want to tell Mrs. Guggenheim."

"Then the steward produced a piece of paper. He had written the message on it, he said, to be certain that it would be correct.

"That's all he said," added the steward, "there wasn't time for more."

Into the Darkness

Little by little Mr. Guggenheim got the account of his brother's death from the steward. It was the first definite news that he had received of his brother.

"Mr. Guggenheim was one of my charges," said the steward. "He had his secretary with him. His name was Giglio, I believe, an Armenian, about twenty-four years old. Both died like men.

"When the crash came, I awakened them and told them to get dressed. A few minutes later I went into their rooms and helped them to get ready. I put a life preserver on Mr. Guggenheim. He said it hurt him in the back. There was plenty of time and I took it off, adjusted it, and then put it on.

"They wanted to get out on deck with only a few clothes on, but I pulled a heavy sweater over Mr. Guggenheim's life belt, and then they both went out. They stayed together and I could see what they were doing. They were going from one lifeboat to another helping the women and children.

"Mr. Guggenheim would shout out, 'Women first,' and he was of great assistance to the officers.
"Things weren't so bad at first, but when I saw Mr. Guggenheim about three quarters of an hour after the crash there was great excitement. What surprised me was that both Mr. Guggenheim and his secretary were dressed in their evening clothes. They had deliberately taken off their sweaters, and as nearly as I can remember, they wore no life belts at all.

"'What's that for?' I asked.

"'We've dressed up in our best,' replied Mr. Guggenheim, 'and are prepared to go down like gentlemen.' It was then he told me about the message to his wife and that is what I have come with"

Well, shortly after the last few boats were lowered and I was ordered by the deck officer to man an oar, I waved good-bye to Mr. Guggenheim, and that was the last I saw of him and his secretary."

John Jacob Astor

Narratives of the remarkable heroism of Colonel John Jacob Astor and the patient fortitude of Mrs. Astor under conditions that tried the self-control of the hardiest, continue to come to light.

The narrative of the dreadful suspense, which in a short time changed her from a radiant bride to a sorrowing widow, was told by a friend of the family.

At the same time, survivors who occupied lifeboat No. 4, in which Mrs. Astor and her maid escaped, told of how Mrs. Astor had helped calm the other women and had even offered fellow sufferers portions of her slender stock of clothing.

"Mrs. Astor was the bravest little woman I ever met," said Jack Foley, who, with his mate, Sam Parks, pulled an oar in boat No. 4.

"Colonel Astor was a man all through, if there ever was one," continued Foley. "You see, it took us some time to launch boat No. 4. After we had all the women and the children in the boat, we discovered that we couldn't launch her until we removed the sounding spar several decks below.

"So Sam and I got down and chopped the spar away. We were some time doing this, as we had to hunt for an ax.

"We finally got the spar away and launched the boat. That is why boat No. 4 was the last boat to be launched. The others had a free way below it and could be put in the water at once.

"While waiting up there, Mrs. Astor several times wanted to leave the boat. Mr. Astor kept telling the good little woman that he was sure to be saved and that it was her duty to go.

"She stretched out her arms just as though she was pleading with him to let her get out of the boat and take her place with him. Mr. Astor picked up a heavy steamer shawl and wrapped it about her shoulders.

"After pulling those eight men into the boat, I was pretty wet and was shivering, Mrs. Astor threw the shawl about my shoulders and said that I needed it more than she did. I told her that I would get warmed up after pulling a while at the oar and would have no use for it.

"I put the shawl back on her lap," Foley continued. "Sitting next to Mrs. Astor was a Swedish woman with a little girl that I should take to be three or four years old. The little girl was whimpering with the cold. Mrs. Astor took the shawl and threw it about the shoulders of this woman, who thanked her in some foreign lingo. Then the steerage woman kissed her little girl and took her into her arms and wrapped the shawl about her.

"When the explosion occurred aboard the ship, Mrs. Astor made some kind of a sound, but I couldn't understand whether she said anything or merely sobbed. She turned her head away, from the direction of the vessel."

So little was the impact felt at the time of the collision that Mrs. Astor thought the crash was the result of some mishap in the kitchen and paid no attention to it until the engines stopped.

Into the Darkness

Then, realizing that something was wrong, she inquired of her steward the cause. He informed her that a slight accident had happened, and that the captain had ordered the women to the lifeboats, but he added that this was only a precautionary measure, and that they would all be back soon again on the ship.

Mrs. Astor then entered her stateroom and changed her dress, preparatory to leaving the *Titanic* for one of the lifeboats in company with her maid.

As she left the room, the steward told her he would lock up her suite so that nobody would enter it during her absence, for he thought everybody would soon return.

Colonel Astor accompanied his wife and her maid to lifeboat No. 4. When he attempted to enter it, he was pushed back by the sailor in charge, and was told that no men were permitted in it.

"But," said Colonel Astor, "there are no more women to be taken in, and there is plenty of room."

"That makes no difference," replied the man; "the orders are no men, so you cannot get in."

There was no use arguing, Colonel and Mrs. Astor thought, so, waving her adieu, he called out: "Good-bye, Madeleine."

Conflicting accounts of confusion and chaos

Reports that a number of men—probably steerage passengers—on the *Titanic* who tried to rush the lifeboats and preempt the places of women and children were unceremoniously shot were confirmed by Jack Williams and William French, able seamen, survivors of the *Titanic*'s crew.

"When the first of the 56-foot lifeboats were being filled," explained Williams, "the first stampede of panic-stricken men occurred. Within a dozen feet of where I stood I saw fully, ten men throw themselves into the boats already crowded with women and children.

"These men were dragged back and hurled sprawling across the deck. Six of them, screaming with fear, struggled to their feet and made a second attempt to rush the boats.

"About ten shots sounded in quick succession. The six cowardly men were stopped in their tracks, staggered and collapsed one after another. At least two of them vainly attempted to creep toward the boats again. The others lay quite still. This scene of bloodshed served its purpose. In that particular section of the deck, there was no further attempt to violate the 'women and children first' rule."

"Were any of these men from the first or second cabins?" Williams was asked.

Williams passed the query on to his sailor chum French, who replied:

"It was hard to tell. All of them were so scantily dressed. In the semi-darkness and prevailing excitement, faces left no distinct impression with me. I should say that most, if not all of them, were from the steerage.

"Other men passengers, who in a general way resemble these same men, were among a score or so who jumped from the upper decks into the boats occupied by women and children after the order had been given to lower boats. These men were not shot. They were tossed by the officers and crew of the boat into the sea, where most of them perished, as they deserved to.

"The report that First Officer Murdock and not Captain Smith, shot himself on the bridge just as the forward section of the *Titanic* sank is true. I still have before me the picture of Mr. Murdock standing on the bridge as the waters surged up about him, placing the pistol to his head and disappearing as the shot that ended his life rang out."

Williams continued: "A lot had been printed in the papers about the heroism of the officers, but little has been said of the bravery of the men below the decks. I was told that 17 enginemen, who were drowned side by side, got down on their knees on the platform of the engine room and prayed until the water surged up to their necks.

"Then they stood up clasped hands so as to form a circle and died together. All of these men helped rake the fires out from ten of the forward boilers after the crash. This delayed the explosion and undoubtedly permitted the ship to remain afloat nearly an hour longer, and thus saved hundreds of lives."

Richard Norris Williams, Jr.

According to Richard Norris Williams, Jr., his father, C. Duane Williams, was killed, not drowned, in the *Titanic* wreck.

The son said his father was crushed to death by a falling funnel. His account of the tragedy was given through Mrs. Alexander Williams, daughter-in-law of his uncle, Richard Norris Williams.

"Richard told us," she said, "that he and his father had been watching the *Titanic*'s lifeboats lowered and filled with women. The water was up to their waists and the ship was about at her last few minutes.

Into the Darkness

"Suddenly one of the great funnels fell. Richard sprang aside, trying to drag his father after him. But Mr. Williams was caught under the funnel. A moment later, the funnel was swept overboard, and the decks were cleared of water. Mr. Williams, the father, had disappeared.

"Richard sprang overboard and swam through the ice to a life raft. He was pulled aboard. There were five other men there and one woman. Occasionally they were swept off into the sea, even the woman, but they always managed to climb back. Finally those on the raft were picked up by a *Titanic* lifeboat, and later were saved by the *Carpathia*."

Young Mr. Williams said he didn't see Bruce Ismay, managing director of the White Star Line, after the iceberg was struck. He didn't know the Wideners or other Philadelphians aboard when he saw them.

Chapter 11 — Carpathia Arrives to a Horrifying Scene

In the hours after the *Titanic* sank, the press was faced with the task of telling a story about what had been thought impossible—the sinking of an unsinkable ship. Without substantive information—before the rescuing *Carpathia* returned to the United States—news bureaus around the world started running speculative accounts about the disaster.

For four days, as the *Carpathia* sailed to New York from the site of the sinking, carrying her original vacationing passengers and newly boarded *Titanic* survivors, three men—each instrumental to our knowledge of the event today—were embedded in one of the century's most shocking stories: Arthur Rostron, English captain of the *Carpathia*; Lawrence Beesley, English scientist and *Titanic* survivor; and Carlos Hurd, an American reporter and *Carpathia* passenger who had been on vacation with his wife. Their sense of the tragedy, and their response to the news world during the days that followed, show us the different ways that individuals define and experience extreme trauma.

Into the Darkness

Carpathia Capt. Arthur Henry Rostron

In all of his years at sea, Arthur Rostron, 40 years old, had never needed to respond to a distress call. He had 23 years of naval experience, but was captain of the *Carpathia* for only three months when he was roused by Harold Cottam, his ship's radio operator, in the early hours of April 15, 1912. Cottam awoke an annoyed Rostron in his cabin to convey the frantic QCD (or Quick Come Distress) call from the *Titanic*: "Hurry, Hurry! ... "sinking by the head."

Captain Rostron responded immediately—moving full speed ahead toward the accident site. By the time the *Carpathia* arrived at the *Titanic*'s last reported location, Rostron had organized his ship and readied its passengers for the hysteria he anticipated. Electric lights were rigged along the *Carpathia*; gangway doors were opened; pilot ladders, nets, and ropes were ready to be dropped; hot drinks, soup, warm clothing, and blankets were on deck. Cargo cranes were ready to haul in the mail and the passengers' luggage. The three doctors on board were set up at first aid stations in the ship's dining rooms.

The entire crew of the *Carpathia* was assembled on deck and were told of what had happened. The chief steward, Harry Hughes, told them what was expected of them.

"Every man to his post and let him do his full duty like a true Englishman," he said. "If the situation calls for it, let us add another glorious page to British history."

Into the Darkness

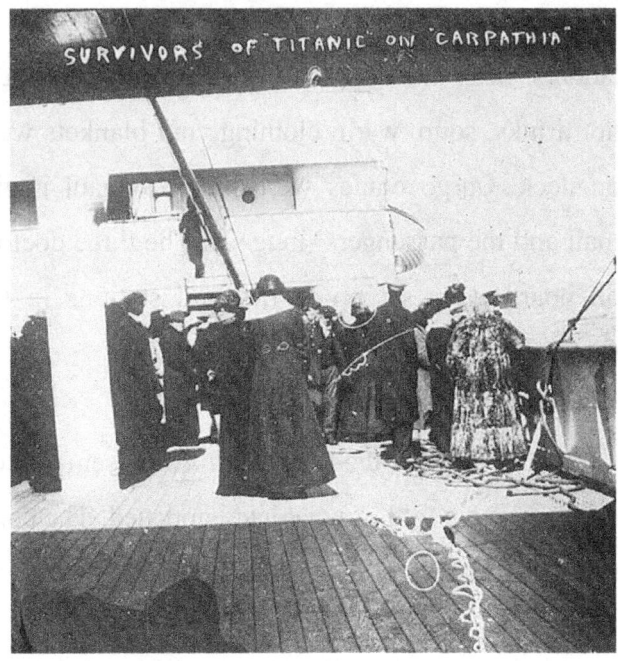

**Detail from a photo showing the survivors of the Titanic on the rescue ship Carpathia,
from the Bain News Service, 1912.**

After that every man saluted and went to his post. There was no confusion. Everything was in readiness for the reception of the survivors before 2 o'clock. Only one or two of the passengers were on deck, one of them, Mr. Beachler, having been awakened by a friend, and the other because of inability to sleep. Many of the *Carpathia*'s passengers slept all through the morning up to 10 o'clock, and had no idea of what was going on.

At 4:00 a.m., arriving at the *Titanic*'s last reported position, Captain Rostron stopped the *Carpathia*, shut down its engines—and felt sick. He saw nothing. No ship. No lights. No lifeboats or passengers. Nothing. Moments later, however, he spotted a dim green light on the horizon—a lifeboat with two passengers aboard. As the first survivor boarded the *Carpathia*, she confirmed to the stunned crew the shocking, horrific truth: the *Titanic* had sunk. As daylight broke, several lifeboats and a number of icebergs filled Rostron's view.

Into the Darkness

With icebergs visible in every direction, Rostron, a religious man, would later look back at the *Carpathia*'s speedy rescue dash and say that he, like the captain of the *Titanic,* was moving dangerously fast through the icebergs that morning, and the only thing to save his ship from being sliced open like the *Titanic* was "the hand of God."

Lawrence Beesley, the rescued English scientist who had been a second-class *Titanic* passenger, described the morning of April 15 in his memoir *The Loss of the S.S. Titanic:*

As far as the eye could reach to the north and west lay an unbroken stretch of field of ice, with icebergs still attached to the floe and rearing aloft their mass as a hill might suddenly rise from a level plain. Ahead and to the south and east huge floating monsters were showing up through the waning darkness, their number added to moment by moment as the dawn broke and flushed the horizon pink.

It is remarkable how "busy" all those icebergs made the sea look: to have gone to bed with nothing but sea and sky and to come on deck to find so many objects in the sight made quite a change in the character of the sea: it looked quite crowded; and a lifeboat alongside and people clambering aboard, mostly women, in nightdresses and dressing-gowns, in cloaks and shawls, in anything but ordinary clothes! Out ahead and on all sides little torches glittered faintly for a few moments and then guttered out—and shouts and cheers floated across the quiet sea. It would be difficult to imagine a more unexpected sight than this that lay before the Carpathia's passengers as they line the sides that morning in the early dawn...

"The first lifeboat reached the Carpathia about half-past 5 o'clock in the morning, and the last of the sixteen boats was unloaded before 9 o'clock. Some of the lifeboats were only half filled, the first one having but two men and eleven women, when it had accommodations for at least forty. There were few men in the boats. The women were the gamest lot I have ever seen. Some of the men and women were in evening clothes, and others among those saved had nothing on but night clothes and raincoats."

Beesley continued: "As soon as they were landed on the Carpathia many of the women became hysterical, but on the whole they behaved splendid. Men and women appeared to be stunned all day Monday, the full force of the disaster not reaching them until Tuesday night. After being wrapped up in blankets and given brandy and hot coffee, their first thoughts were for their husbands and those at home."

"Most of them imagined that their husbands had been picked up by other vessels and then began flooding the wireless rooms with messages. We knew that those who were not on board the Carpathia had gone down to death, and this belief was confirmed Monday afternoon when we received a wire from Mr. Marconi himself asking why no news had been sent."

"We knew that if any other vessel could by any chance have picked them up it would have communicated with land. After a while, when the survivors failed to get any answer to their queries, they grew so restless that Captain Rostrom posted a notice that all private messages had been sent and that the wireless had not been used to give information to the press, as had been charged. Little

by little it began to dawn on the women on board, and most of them guessed the worst before they reached here. I saw Mrs. John Jacob Astor when she was taken from the lifeboat. She was calm and collected. She kept to her stateroom all the time, leaving it only to attend a meeting of the survivors on Tuesday afternoon."

By 8:30 a.m., with survivors on board and their lifeboats hauled on deck, Captain Rostron surveyed the exact site of the *Titanic*'s descent. All that remained of the once marvelous, unsinkable ship was a dense litter field of floating debris. Rostron asked an Episcopalian minister aboard to lead a service that morning—a prayer "out of respect to those who were lost and of gratitude for those who were saved." In over four hours of searching the vicinity, Captain Rostron saw only one body floating on the ocean's surface.

Rostron made sure *Carpathia* passengers would be segregated from *Titanic* survivors. He established a check-in process to create adequate documentation as survivors boarded. He told his crew to drink coffee before they had reached the disaster, warning it was going to be a long night ahead. Starting at 2:45 a.m., Rostron had the *Carpathia* blast "encouragement rockets" every 15 minutes to signal *Titanic* passengers and crew that help was on the way.

Carlos Hurd

Earlier that morning, Carlos Hurd, an American news reporter for the St. Louis Post-Dispatch, and his wife were second-class *Carpathia* passengers, traveling on vacation from the U.S. to Fiume (now Croatia). Hurd was awakened by a strange feeling. His cabin was cold, and the *Carpathia* was not moving. Confused by the silence of the engines and the clamor of hallway voices, he decided to investigate. He walked to what was the dining room the evening before but that morning appeared to be an infirmary. A *Carpathia* crewmember, pointing to a disheveled group of shivering refugees in the makeshift hospital, broke the news to Hurd: "From the *Titanic*; she's at the bottom of the ocean."

Carlos Hurd

From the *Carpathia's* deck, Hurd then saw a number of approaching lifeboats filled with traumatized survivors. As they boarded—numb and in shock, and searching for loved companions—Carlos Hurd stopped his vacation and got to work.

Finding any scraps of paper he could, he began to interview survivors, many of whom were devastated women and children. Immigrants whose life savings fell to the bottom of the sea, women who could not speak English, all now were being towed to a new world without the men who had been guiding their futures. Hurd wrote down their various, sometimes contradictory, accounts of the *Titanic's* descent.

One survivor said *Titanic* Captain Smith was last sighted standing atop the sinking ship's bridge, as her decks washed away, before jumping into the sea—with no life preserver evident—and swimming away from a rescue attempt. Another account claimed Smith had shot himself on board as the ship went down. Hurd wrote of both accounts.

Yes, the *Titanic*'s string band played until the ship's last moments. However, based on Hurd's record of the sentiment of survivors, who, hearing the music, knowing the words of the last ballad—"So by my woes I'll be, Nearer my God, to Thee"—some watching loved ones clinging to the rails of the sinking ship or flailing helplessly in the frigid sea—the music brought out more "strain" than relief. The combination of the music, the wretched groans of death, the beauty of the stars above, and the horrendous sight of the ship slowly ripping in two before sinking was too much to bear.

From surviving *Titanic* quartermaster J.H. Moody, Hurd obtained some reasons for the accident. The *Titanic* had been moving full steam ahead, ignoring warnings from other vessels about the presence of icebergs. The trip was less a maiden voyage and more a race to reach New York in the best time. According to Moody, "...officers were striving to live up to the orders to smash the record."

In his account Beesley took issue with the way survivors were portrayed by the press, believing the scene on the *Carpathia* was intentionally overblown for effect. He felt his own sense of the survivors' states of mind was much more truthful than the press's depiction:

"Much that is exaggerated and false has been written about the mental condition of passengers as they came aboard: we have been described as being too dazed to understand what was happening, as being too overwhelmed to speak, and as looking before us with 'set, staring gaze' with the shadow of the dread event....scenes of women weeping and

brooding over their losses hour by hour until they were driven mad by grief—all this has been reported to the press by people on board the Carpathia...the one thing that matters in describing an event of this kind is the exact truth...and my own impression of our mental condition is that of supreme gratitude and relief at treading the firm decks of a ship again."

On board the *Carpathia*, Beesley and other *Titanic* survivors formed a committee to establish, among other things, a general fund for survivors from steerage, to present a loving cup to Captain Rostron, and to write a public letter suggesting better safeguards for ocean travel. Beesley felt it critical to accurately describe the accident—"to inform the English public"—and to bring perspective to the American press's histrionic tendencies in reporting disasters:

Into the Darkness

"It seemed well, too, while on the Carpathia to prepare as accurate an account as possible of the disaster and to have this ready for the press, in order to calm public opinion and to forestall the incorrect and hysterical accounts which some American reporters are in the habit of preparing on occasions of this kind. The first impression is often and most permanent, and in a disaster of this magnitude, where exact and accurate information is so necessary, preparation of a report was essential. It was written in odd corners of the deck and saloon of the Carpathia, and fell, it seemed very happily, into the hands of the one reporter who could best deal with it, the Associated Press. I understand it was the first report that came through and had a good deal of the effect intended."

As the *Carpathia* made its way back to its harbor with Hurd, Beesley, and the survivors on board, the fate of the *Titanic* was unknown to newsrooms around the world. A number of papers ran speculative accounts of what had happened: There was an accident, and the *Titanic* and all its passengers were being towed back to safety; the amazing *Titanic* sank but all on board were safe; the *Titanic* hit an iceberg and all passengers died at sea.

Meanwhile, on board the *Carpathia*, Captain Rostron had forbidden his crew from talking to reporter Carlos Hurd. In addition, Hurd was not allowed to send his press dispatches via the ship's wireless telegraph. In fact, although Rostron testified later that "absolutely no censorship" took place, much of the communication from the *Carpathia* was held back. In addition, messages to the *Carpathia* from the press on the mainland were intercepted.

Joseph Pulitzer, Hurd's boss at the time, knew that Hurd was on board the *Carpathia,* and sent several radio messages to the *Carpathia* urging Hurd to interview *Titanic* survivors. Charles E. Chapin, city editor of New York's *Evening World,* also knew Hurd was on board, and wanted to run Hurd's first-hand story immediately upon the *Carpathia's* return. Chapin had attempted to send a message to Hurd, asking the reporter to throw his dispatch from the ship's deck to Chapin who would be in a tug boat in New York Harbor as the *Carpathia* arrived.

Hurd never received any of these messages. In fact, Rostron had all messages intercepted and, in effect, had instituted a media blackout on his ship. Rostron apparently went so far as to confiscate all stationery aboard the *Carpathia* so that the reporter would be unable to capture accounts. Hurd was resourceful, using toilet paper, among other items, to write his story. His wife, who was also writing about the surviving women, took her husband's scraps, accumulating shards of chronicles, which she brought to the bed in their cabin and sat on to avoid confiscation.

On the evening of April 18, 1912, the *Carpathia* approached New York. By this time, Carlos Hurd understood he would never be allowed to leave the ship with his story. As the New York lights became evident in a storm-filled sky, a number of tug boats filled with reporters approached the *Carpathia*.

Hearing Hurd's name being called through a megaphone from a tug, the *Carpathia*'s officers ordered Hurd to stay away from the rails. Ignoring their command, Hurd wrapped his story in a cigar box, sealed it closed, and attached champagne corks to the outside. Spotting Chapin in a tug, Hurd chucked the cigar box over the side of the

Carpathia towards the city editor, but the box became ensnared in guy wires securing a *Titanic* lifeboat to the *Carpathia*. A sailor aboard the *Carpathia*, watching the drama unfold, worked his way to where the boxed dispatch had been snagged, grabbed the box, and threw it on to Chapin's tug to the cheers of the *Titanic* survivors.

Into the Darkness

Carpathia Refuses to Give Out Any Word of Closing Hours of the Liner Titanic

All Requests for Details of Collision and Sinking of Ship Are Ignored

CENSORSHIP APPEARS TO BE COMPLETE

No Response Is Given to Inquiries As to What Had Taken Place After the Great Steamer Hit the Iceberg

---

REFUSES TO O. K. MESSAGE.

NEW YORK, April 18.—A wireless message picked up at 2:35 o'clock this morning by the Brooklyn navy yard, sent by the scout cruiser Salem to Siasconsett, said:

"I can read the Carpathia, but he won't take any business from me." The Brooklyn operator said he also heard the Salem tell Siasconsett that he had sent President Taft's message concerning Major Archibald Butt to the Carpathia, but that the wireless operator on the Canarder would not give him an O. K. for it.

Beyond even the mystery of how the Titanic met her fate, another mystery evolved by the events of the last three days forced itself to the front last night.

Although the rescue ship Carpathia was within the zone of wireless communication for hours in the night and both shore stations and relaying ships were able to obtain from her long lists of survivors among the steerage passengers and to send and receive numerous short messages from and to private individuals, not a word of matter descriptive of the manner in which the Titanic received her death blow or how those on board the doomed liner conducted themselves in the face of impending death reached the shore.

From the Idaho Daily Statesman, April 19, 1912

Beesley also described the media's presence as the *Carpathia* entered New York Harbor:

Surrounded by tugs of every kind, from which (as well as from every available building near the river) magnesium bombs were shot off by photographers, while reporters shouted for news of the disaster and photographs of passengers, the Carpathia drew slowly to her station at the Cunard pier, the gangways were pushed across, and we set foot at last on American soil, very thankful, grateful people.

Carlos Hurd's 5,000 word chronicle was immediately published, as were his wife's interviews with *Titanic* survivors. Many New York papers ran first-hand accounts of what had happened aboard the *Titanic* in special editions on the day of the *Carpathia*'s arrival in New York. Hurd's notoriety as a dedicated journalist who stopped at nothing to write of the tragedy of the century followed him for years to come. Captain Arthur Rostron received a number of prestigious awards for his rescue dash to the *Titanic* survivors. And, two months after its sinking, Lawrence Beesley's memoir, *The Loss of the SS Titanic*, was published.

Beesley's and Rostron's apprehension about the role of the American press in such a major world event may have represented a general British regard for U.S. media. London, after all, was the hub of global news up until the sinking of the *Titanic*. Had the *Carpathia* picked up the survivors and brought them back to England, rather than New York, what would have become of Carlos Hurd's story? Would Captain Rostron have been more cooperative about news dispatches coming and going to his ship if the correspondence to the *Carpathia* had come from London? Did New York newspapers become an established voice of international news simply because the *Carpathia* delivered the survivors of the *Titanic* to the news reporters of New York rather than London?

What is to be made of Lawrence Beesley's sense that there was minimal drama in the immediate aftermath of the wreck of the century—an accident in which only 31 percent of those on board survived, and those survivors witnessed the stunning, horrific loss of so many lives? How could Beesley describe the response of survivors as reflecting "gratitude" and "relief," without any prevalence of shock and hysteria on board the *Carpathia*? What effect does one's cultural identity have on information portrayed—or not portrayed—during an epic international tragedy? Does a calamity really have an "exact truth," as Beesley set out to provide in his memoir, or do multiple, disjointed, perspectives, such as those coming from Carlos Hurd, Captain Rostron, and Lawrence Beesley, give us a better understanding of the wreck of the *Titanic* and its aftermath?

Dr. J.F. Kemp

Dr. J.F. Kemp, the *Carpathia*'s physician, told the story of how a snap decision by the wireless operator on the *Carpathia*, was instrumental to the rescue even taking place.

"Our wireless operator," said Dr. Kemp, "was about to retire Sunday night when he said, jokingly: 'I guess I'll wait just ten minutes, then turn in.'

"It was in the next ten minutes that the *Titanic*'s call for help came. Had the wireless man not waited, there would have been no survivors.

"I had turned in for the night when Main, our wireless operator, caught the 'S0S' signal of distress," said Dr. Kemp. "He told me it was the clearest signal of any sort he ever received. The minute he got the message he hastened to Captain Rostrom and said, 'Captain, the *Titanic* is sinking; she struck an iceberg.' Captain Rostrom did not believe it. 'Here it comes again, Captain,' said the operator.

"That was all the captain needed to get our crew into action; he sounded the bell for the watchman, and sent him to order all hands on deck.

"I doubt if any passengers on the *Carpathia* knew of the tragedy until Jones, the first mate, sounded the emergency gong after the watchman had summoned the crew.

"A few minutes after we got the signal for help we were ready for action," said Dr. Kemp. "The S0S reached us shortly after midnight. We were then 56 miles away from the *Titanic*. Our engineer turned about and put on full speed, and we reached the *Titanic* about 3.30 o'clock Monday morning."

Dr. Kemp continued: "While the *Carpathia* was speeding toward the doomed ship, Captain Rostrom summoned the higher officers together, and said he would hold every man responsible for the work assigned to him.

"He told Main to answer the *Titanic* and tell Captain Smith that we were making for his ship, full steam ahead.

"Phillips, the wireless operator of the *Titanic*, evidently did not get our reply, or, if he did receive it, he could not answer us in any way. Captain Rostrom told Mrs. Smith, the stewardess, to prepare for any emergency. He told her to get coffee, sandwiches and other food ready for the survivors.

Into the Darkness

"On our way to the *Titanic,* the captain went below and told the engineer that he must get to the *Titanic* before she sank. I doubt if Captain Rostrom ever got as much speed out of the *Carpathia* as he did on the way to the *Titanic.*"

Dr. Kemp continued: "Long before the *Carpathia* got near the scene of the wreck, our boats were ready to be lowered into the water.

"Two men were stationed at each boat, and I and Thomas McKenna, seaman, were in charge of boat No. 1. We have sixteen boats on the ship, and they were hanging suspended from the davits within 15 minutes after we received the SOS call for help.

"I must not forget the women who were on the *Carpathia*. They were the most self-sacrificing women I ever saw. Their fortitude under the distressing circumstances was so remarkable that each one ought to be rewarded for the work she did after the survivors were lifted aboard the *Carpathia*," Dr. Kemp said.

"As we got near the scene of the wreck the barometer dropped considerably. It became cold — bitter cold. We did not see the icebergs then, but Captain Rostrom said that we were nearing them. Suddenly, as the iceberg loomed up ahead of our ship, Captain Rostrom ran to the pilot house and took charge of the helm.

"The night was clear and starlight, but we did not see an iceberg until the *Carpathia* was within a half mile of it. Of course, we had ample time to steer clear of the floes.

"At 3.30 o'clock our vessel plunged into a sea of open ice. I believe there must have been thirty or forty icebergs in the water around the *Carpathia*.

Into the Darkness

Captain Rostrom took his ship safely through the floe and suddenly we heard a shriek. It was faint at first and then it became louder.

"'The women and children, get them first,' Captain Rostrom shouted to the crew on the boat deck who were awaiting the signal to cut loose lifeboats. Our searchlight was trained on the sea ahead and the boats filled with the shipwrecked passengers stood out in bold relief," Dr. Kemp said.

"I shall never forget the sight. There were many boats from the *Titanic* loaded with women and children wedged among the ice. Even before we got up to the first boat from the *Titanic,* we could see the iceberg which sank her. It looked to be as big as the Rock of Gibraltar. It towered high in the air and it moved very slowly.

"I believe it was over 500 feet high, and we can judge by its size by recalling that seven-eighths of an iceberg is submerged. Within fifty yards of the boats in the water Captain Rostrom gave the signal to reverse the engines so our ship would not crash into the shipwrecked passengers.

"'Ready men—go,' shouted the captain to me, and McKenna loosened the rope and our boat dropped into the water. We tugged away at the oars with all our strength. We shoved our boat alongside of boat No. 13 from the *Titanic*. It was filled with passengers. I believe there were about fifteen children in it."

Dr. Kemp continued: "Poor little things! Some were benumbed with cold; others were apparently lifeless, and several moaned piteously. The women in the boat were scantily clad. Their clothing was grotesque. They had on wraps, night robes, silk shawls ever their heads and men's coats around them. Many had no shoes, and all of them suffered from the cold.

"McKenna and I tied a hawser to the boat and then rowed back to the *Carpathia*. Harris, the bos'n's mate, and another member of the crew helped us to lift the unfortunate ones from the boat. Some had to be carried up the ladder to the boat deck of the *Carpathia*.

"A few could walk, but the majority were so benumbed that they could neither speak nor walk.

"As fast as others of our crew could get the *Titanic*'s boats they were dragged toward the side of the *Carpathia*. We rescued twenty boatloads of passengers—710 in all. Our ship resembled a hospital on our way back to New York, for a number of the women and children were ill.

"The three physicians on the *Carpathia* told me as we were going up the bay that there were sixteen patients for the hospital as soon as the *Carpathia* docked."

Carpathia crew prepares for the worst

A steward from the *Carpathia* told the following tale of the rescue of the *Titanic*'s passengers and crew to a group of his mates:

"It was between quarter after and half after 1 o'clock, ship's time, Monday morning," he said, "when all the stewards were mustered and Chief Steward Highes told us that a wireless had just come in that the *Titanic* had hit an iceberg and probably would need help. He urged us to turn right in and get ready for a ship's load of people. The *Carpathia* turned in the direction the wireless had called from.

Into the Darkness

"We got hot coffee ready and laid out blankets and made sandwiches and everything like that. It seemed as if every passenger on the boat knew about the trouble and turned out. Captain Rostrom had shut off the hot water all over the ship and turned every ounce of heat into steam, and the old boat was as excited as any of us.

"After we got things ready we went out on deck. It was a glorious morning—no swell in the sea, but bitter cold. The ship's lights were on full blaze and we were there in the middle of a sea of ice—the finest sight I ever saw.

The *Carpathia* steward continued: "Just as it was about half day and dark we came upon a boat. There were eighteen men in it and it was in charge of an officer. There were no women in the boat, and it was not more than one-third filled. All of the men were able to come up the Jacob's ladder on the *Carpathia*, which we threw over the port side.

Every one of them was given some brandy or hot black coffee. After they were all on board we pulled up their boat.

"It was bright morning by now and all around the *Carpathia*, here and there, about a quarter mile apart, were more boats. These were fuller than the first and there were women in all of them. The women were hoisted up in bo'suns chairs, and the men who could do so climbed the Jacob's ladder. Some of the men, however, had to be hauled up, especially the firemen. There was a whole batch of firemen saved. They were nearly naked. They had jumped overboard and swam after the boats, it turned out, and they were almost frozen stiff.

"The women were dressed, and the funny thing about it is only five of them had to be taken to the hospital. Both the men's hospitals were filled—twenty-four beds in all. We got twelve boatloads, I think, inside of a little more than an hour. Then, between quarter after and half after 8 o'clock, we got the last two boats—crowded to the guards and almost all women.

"After we got the last boatload aboard, the *Californian* came alongside and the captains arranged that we should make straight for New York and the *Californian* would look around for more boats. We circled round and round, though, and we saw all kinds of wreckage. There was not a person on a stick of it and we did not get sight of another soul.

The steward continued: "While we were pulling in, the boatloads of women we saved were quiet enough and not making any trouble at all. But when it seemed sure we would not find any more persons alive then bedlam came.

"I hope I never go through it again. The way those women took on for the folks they had lost was awful and we could not do anything to quiet them until they cried themselves out.

"There were five Chinamen in the boats and not a soul knew where they came from. No one saw them get into the boats; but there they were—wherever they came from.

"The fellows from the crew of the *Titanic* told us that lots more of them could have got away, only no one would believe that their ship could sink."

Survivors reach New York

The arrival of the *Carpathia* brought a vast multitude of people to the Cunard docks. They filled the vast pier sheds, and, overflowing for blocks, crowded the nearby streets in a dense throng. Through it all the rain fell steadily, adding a funeral aspect to the scene. The landing of the survivors was attended with little excitement, the crowd standing in awe-like silence as the groups from the ship passed along.

The docking actually began shortly after nine o'clock and the debarking of passengers was so quickly disposed of by the waiving of the usual formality that practically everything had been concluded by 10.30 o'clock. The crowds remained about the pier long after this, however, to get a glimpse of the rescuing steamer and to hear the harrowing stories, which had been brought back by the ship.

The Rev. P.M.A. Hoque, a Catholic priest of St. Cesare, Canada, who was a passenger on the *Carpathia*, told of finding the boats containing the survivors.

"Every woman and child, as if by instinct, put the loops around their bodies and drew them taut. Some of the women climbed the ladders. To others, chairs were lowered and in these they were lifted aboard.

"Not a word was spoken by any one of the rescued or the rescuers. Everybody was too be-numbed by horror to speak. It was a time for action and not words.

"Not a tear dimmed the eyes of one of the hundreds we got on deck. The women were less excited than the men. Apparently, they all had drained their tear ducts dry, for every eye was red and swollen."

Dr. Alice Leeder

One of the most interesting accounts of the *Titanic* disaster came to light in a letter written on board the *Carpathia* by Dr. Alice Leeder, of New York, one of the survivors, after she had been transferred to the *Carpathia* in a lifeboat.

The letter is a personal communication addressed to Mrs. Sarah Babcock, of Philadelphia. By the wavering of the handwriting, one can readily realize the state of mind in which it was written.

In the letter Dr. Leeder said there was no panic on board the *Titanic*, and that everyone who had to meet death met it with composure. She speaks of the generosity and kindness shown by the crew and passengers of the *Carpathia* in their treatment of the survivors. Following is the letter:

Royal Mail Steamship Carpathia,

Into the Darkness

Wednesday, April 16

My Dear Mrs. Babcock:

We have been through a most terrible experience—the Titanic and above a thousand souls sunk on Monday about 3 o'clock in the morning. Margaret and I are safe, although we have lost everything. One of our party, also, Mr. Kenyon, was lost. He was such a charming man—so honorable and good.

I sat talking to him a little before the accident—and a little later he was dead. His wife is crushed by the blow. I can say one thing, nothing could part me from my husband in time of danger.

After floating about for four hours, we were taken on board the steamer that was bound for Naples—but she is now taking us New York.

Into the Darkness

It is terrible to see the people who have lost their families and friends—one lady has lost $15,000 worth of clothing, and no one has saved anything. Many of the passengers have only their night clothes with coats over them.

I shall never forget the sight of that beautiful boat as she went down, the orchestra playing to the last, the lights burning until they were extinguished by the waves. It sounds so unreal, like a scene on the stage. We were hit by an iceberg.

We were in the midst of a field of ice; towers of ice; fantastic shapes of ice! It is all photographed on my mind. There was no panic. Everyone met death with composure—as one said, the passengers were a set of thoroughbreds.

We are moving slowly toward New York. Everyone on this boat is so kind to us. Clothing and all the necessaries are at our convenience. I am attired in my old blue serge, a steamer hat; truth to tell, I am a sorry looking object to land in New York.

This is rather a mixed up epistle, but please pardon lack of clearness of expression. If you want me, some time I will come to Philadelphia for a day or two in the future.

With dear love,

Alice J. Leeder

Chapter 12 — Criticism of Titanic's Preparedness

The urgent need of lifeboat drills on the trans-Atlantic liner was touched upon by Mrs. William R. Bucknell, widow of the founder of Bucknell University, and herself one of the survivors of the disaster.

Mrs. Bucknell said that not only were the passengers on the *Titanic* absolutely unfamiliar with the life-saving equipment of the vessel, but that the equipment was inadequate and even faulty.

The lifeboats were bunglingly fastened to their davits, she said, and many of the collapsibles were too stiff to open and thus useless for service.

To her, the greatest crime was the "unpreparedness" of the lifeboat equipment. Mrs. Bucknell declared one of the boats was launched with the plug out of the bottom, and afterwards sank, the occupants fortunately being rescued by the *Titanic*'s fifth officer.

The lifeboat in which she was placed by Captain Smith, she declared, was manned only by a steward and three ordinary seamen. And none of the men, she declared, knew how to row.

Mrs. Bucknell also said that she had not seen a lifeboat drill while she was aboard the *Titanic*, and diligent inquiry among those rescued, after they were safely aboard the *Carpathia*, failed to develop any knowledge on their part of such drills ever having been held.

Mrs. Bucknell said that the only provisions aboard her lifeboat was a basket full of bread. She saw no water, although she said that two small casks beneath one of the seats may have contained water.

"The lifeboats were so bunglingly fastened to the davits in the first place that it was hard work to get them free," she said.

"Half the collapsible boats were so stiff that they could not be opened and were useless. Those that were not already opened and ready for use were unavailable, also, for none on board seemed to understand how they worked. Hundreds more could have been saved if these collapsible boats had worked properly.

"I was asleep in my cabin when the crash came," said Mrs. Bucknell, beginning her account of the disaster. "I cannot explain just what the noise was like, except that it was horrible and sounded like a mixture of thunder and explosions.

"In a moment, there was a roaring sound and I knew that something serious was the matter. The corridors filled rapidly with frightened passengers and then the stewards and officers came, reassuring us with the announcement that everything was all right and that only a small hole had been stove in the bow.

"As I stepped out of my stateroom, I saw lying before me on the floor a number of fragments of ice as big as my fists. More was crumbled about the porthole, and it flashed over me at once just what had happened.

"'We have hit an iceberg,' I said to my maid, 'get dressed at once.'

"We hurried into our clothes, and I took the precaution to get fully dressed. So did my maid. I even thought to wrap myself in my warm fur coat, for even then I felt sure we would have to take to the boats. Something told me the damage was greater than we had been told.

"My fears were realized a few minutes later when a steward walked briskly down the corridor, calling to the passengers who had retired again to hurry into their clothes and get on deck at once. I could see by this man's drawn and haggard face that something dreadful had happened."

Mrs. Bucknell continued: "There was very little confusion on the deck. Once a group of men shouted that they would not be separated from their wives and made a rush to find accommodations for themselves. The captain seemed to straighten out his shoulders and his face was set with determination.

"'Get back there, you cowards,' he roared. 'Behave yourself like men. Look at these women. Can you not be as brave as they?'

"The men fell back, and from that moment there seemed to be a spirit of resignation all over the ship. Husbands and wives clasped each other and burst into tears. Then a few minutes later came the order for the women and children to take to the boats.

"I did not hear an outcry from the women or the men. Wives left their husbands' side and without a word were led to the boats. One little Spanish girl, a bride, was the only exception.

"She wept bitterly, and it was almost necessary to drag her into the boat. Her husband went down with the ship.

"The last person I remember seeing was Colonel Astor. When he had been told by the captain that it would be impossible for the husbands to take to the boats with their wives, he took Mrs. Astor by the arm and they walked quietly away to the other side of the vessel. As we pulled away, I saw him leaning tenderly over her, evidently whispering words of comfort.

"There were 35 persons in the boat in which the captain placed me. Three of them were ordinary seamen, supposed to manage the boat, and a steward.

"One of these men seemed to think that we should not start from the sinking ship until it could be learned whether the other boats would accommodate the rest of the women. He seemed to think that more could be crowded into ours, if necessary.

"'I would rather go back and go down with the ship than leave under these circumstances,' he cried."

Mrs. Bucknell continued: "We rowed all night. I took an oar and sat beside the Countess de Rothes. Her maid had an oar and so did mine. The air was freezing cold, and it was not long before the only man that appeared to know anything about rowing commenced to complain that his hands were freezing.

"A woman back of him handed him a shawl from about her shoulders.

"As we rowed we looked back at the lights of the *Titanic*. There was not a sound from her, only the lights began to get lower and lower, and finally she sank. Then we heard a muffled explosion and a dull roar caused by the great suction of water.

Into the Darkness

"There was not a drop of water on our boat. The last minute before our boat was launched Captain Smith threw a bag of bread aboard. I took the precaution of taking a good drink of water before we started, so I suffered no inconvenience from thirst.

"Another thing that I must not forget to mention, it is but additional proof of my charge that the *Titanic* was poorly equipped. The lamp on our boat was nearly devoid of oil," Mrs. Bucknell said.

"'For God's sake, keep that wick turned down low, or you will be in complete darkness,' we were told on leaving. It wasn't long before these words proved true, and before daylight we were dependent on a cane one of the women had brought along, which contained a tiny electric lamp."

Mrs. Bucknell continued: "With this little glow worm we fought our way through the darkness. I rowed for an hour straight ahead. Then I rested and someone else took my place. Then I grasped the oars again.

"We had rowed about ten miles when looking over Countess Rothe's oar, I spied a faint light to the rear.

"'What's that light?' I almost screamed.

"One of the sailors looked where I indicated and said: 'It's a ship—I can tell by the lights on her masthead.'

"As we passed over the spot where the *Titanic* had gone down we saw nothing but a sheet of yellow scum and a solitary log. There was not a body, not a thing to indicate that there had been a wreck. The sun was shining brightly then, and we were near to the *Carpathia*."

Orchestra plays until the final plunge

George Rheims, of New York, was on the *Titanic* with his brother-in-law, Joseph Holland Loring, of London. He said no one seemed to know for twenty minutes after the boat struck that anything had happened. Many of the passengers stood round for an hour with their life belts on, he said, and saw people getting in the boats.

When all the boats had gone, he added, he shook hands with his brother-in-law, who would not jump, and leaped over the side of the boat.

He swam for a quarter of an hour and reached a boat and climbed in. He found the boat, with eighteen occupants, half under water. The people were in water up to their knees. Seven of them, he said, died during the night.

Of all the heroes who went to their death when the *Titanic* dived to its ocean grave, none, in the opinion of Miss Hilda Slater, a passenger in the last boat to put off, deserved greater credit than the members of the vessel's orchestra. According to Miss Slater, the orchestra played until the last. When the vessel took its final plunge the strains of a lively air mingled gruesomely with the cries of those who realized that they were face to face with death.

Mrs. Alexander T. Compton

Mrs. Alexander T. Compton and her daughter, Miss Alice Compton, of New Orleans, two of the *Titanic*'s rescued, reached New York completely drained with grief over the loss of Mrs. Compton's son, Alexander, who went down with the big liner.

"When we waved good-bye to my son," said Mrs. Compton, "we did not realize the great danger, but thought we were only being sent out in the boats as a precautionary measure. When Captain Smith handed us life preservers, he said cheerily: 'They will keep you warm if you do not have to use them.' Then the crew began clearing the boats and putting the women into them. My daughter and I were lifted in the boat commanded by the fifth officer. There was a moan of agony and anguish from those in our boat when the *Titanic* sank, and we insisted that the officer head back for the place where the *Titanic* had disappeared.

"We found one man with a life preserver on him struggling in the cold water, and for a moment I thought that he was my son."

George Biorden

George Biorden, of California, gave this account:
"I was beside Henry B. Harris, the theatrical manager, when he bade his wife good-bye. Both

started toward the side of the boat where a lifeboat was being lowered.

"Mr. Harris was told it was the rule for women to leave the boat first. 'Yes, I know, I will stay,' Harris said. Shortly after the lifeboats left, a man jumped overboard. Other men followed. It was like sheep following a leader.

"Captain Smith was washed from the bridge into the ocean," Biorden said. "He swam to where a baby was drowning and carried it in his arms while he swam to a lifeboat, which was manned by officers of the *Titanic*. He surrendered the baby to them and swam back to the steamer.

"About the time Captain Smith got back there was an explosion. The entire ship trembled. I had secured a life preserver and jumped over. I struck a piece of ice but was not injured.

"I swam about sixty yards from the steamer when there was a series of explosions. I looked back and saw the *Titanic* go down, bow first. Hundreds of persons were in the water at the time. When the great steamer went down they shrieked hysterically."

Arthur Olsen

Little Arthur Olsen, eight years old, said that America was a pretty good place, and that he was going to like it. Arthur came to that conclusion because so many people had been good to him. First there was Fritzjof Madsen, one of the survivors, who took care of him in the lifeboat.

Then Miss Jean Campbell gave him hot coffee and sandwiches and propped him comfortably against some clothing while she busied herself with others. Later Arthur's stepmother, Mrs. Esther Olson of Brooklyn, appeared and clasped him in her arms.

Her husband, Arthur's father, Charlie Olsen, perished in the wreck.

Mrs. Olsen had never seen Arthur, because after Charlie Oslen's first wife died in Trondhjem, Norway, leaving the little baby Arthur, he had come to America, where he married again. Some time earlier, Olsen had crossed back again to see about the settlement of an estate and to bring his son home. He and the boy were in the steerage of the *Titanic*.

Arthur spoke only Norwegian, but Mrs. Olsen translated for him when he told his story.

"I was with papa on the boat," said the youngster timidly, "and then something was the matter. Papa said I should hurry up and go into the boat and be a good boy. We had a friend, Fritzjof Madsen, with us from our town, and he told me to go too.

Into the Darkness

"The ship was kind of shivering and everybody was running around. We kept getting quite close down to the water, and the water was quiet, like a lake.

"Then I got into a boat and that was all I saw of papa. I saw a lot of people floating around drowning or trying to snatch at our boat. Then all of a sudden I saw Mr. Madsen swimming next to the boat and he was pulled in. He took good care of me.

"In our boat everybody was crying and sighing. I kept very quiet. One man got very crazy, then cried just like a little baby. Another man jumped right into the sea and he was gone.

"It was awful cold in the boat, but I was dressed warm, like we dress in Norway. I had to put on my clothes, when my papa told me to on the big ship. I couldn't talk to anybody, because I don't understand the language. Only Mr. Madsen talked to me and told me not to be afraid, and I wasn't afraid. Mr. Madsen was shivering in his wet clothes, but he got all right after the *Carpathia* came."

Emily Rugg

Miss Emily Rugg, 20 years old, of the Isle of Guernsey, England, told a graphic story of the sinking.

Miss Rugg, who was one of the second class passengers, was on her way to visit relatives. She was asleep when the ship struck the berg, and the jar aroused her. Looking out she saw a mass of ice. Throwing a coat about her, she went on deck and saw lifeboats being lowered.

Returning to the cabin, she dressed, and then went to an adjoining cabin and aroused two women friends. Following this, Miss Rugg ran up on deck and was taken in charge by some of the crew, who dragged her toward a lifeboat. She was lifted into the third from the last which left the ship.

She said that there seemed to be nearly 75 persons in the boat and that it was very much crowded. In the meantime, a panic had started among those who remained on board the *Titanic*.

An Italian jumped from the steerage deck and fell into a lifeboat, landing upon a woman who had a baby in her arms.

Miss Rugg saw the *Titanic* go down and declares but for the horror of it all, it might have been termed one of the grandest sights she ever saw.

"The boat seemed to have broken in half, and with all the lights burning brightly, the stern arose into the air, the lights being extinguished as it did so," she said. "A moment later, the ship plunged beneath the surface."

George A. Harder

George A. Harder, of Brooklyn, N.Y., who, with his bride, was saved from the *Titanic*, told a graphic story of his experience.

"When the crash came, my wife and I were in our stateroom, about to retire," said Harder. "Suddenly there came what seemed like a low, long groan at the ship's bottom. It did not sound like a collision.

"Taking my wife by the arm, I rushed to the deck. Passengers were already swarming there, asking what had happened.

"I heard an officer order a carpenter below to ascertain the damage. He never returned. That the officers already knew the ship was likely to founder was evident from the fact that one lifeboat containing among others Karl M. Behr, the Brooklyn tennis player, had been launched. Persons

Into the Darkness

on our side of the boat—the starboard side—were climbing into a second boat.

"It was a bitter cold night. The stars were bright and their rays were reflected in the surrounding sea, which was as smooth as glass. Farther and farther we drifted away in the lifeboat, leaving behind us the doomed ship.

"Suddenly there sounded from the *Titanic* the strains of 'The Star-Spangled Banner.' As I glanced back at the mighty vessel in the glare of her lights I saw Col. Archibald Gracie clinging to a brass rail near one of the forward funnels. I afterward learned the explosion of the boilers blew him out of the vortex of the sucked-in water to calmer water, where he was rescued.

"Gradually the distance between the *Titanic* and our lifeboat increased. Her lights continued to gleam, her band to play. Two hours later, as she loomed a dark mass on the horizon, her lights suddenly went out. Then across the water, mingling with the strains of 'Nearer, My God, to Thee,' came the distressing cries of those about to die.

"Out of the jumble of foreign tongues could be distinguished the shrieks of steerage women who were grouped at the aft end of the boat. And above all the sounds, like a benediction, sounded that hymn. It was nameless anguish to us to sit in that open boat and realize our helplessness to aid those about to die. We forgot our own losses, our own sufferings. Only a few of us dared to look at the mighty ship as, bow first, she plunged beneath the surface."

Harder denied that many passengers were shot. He said he knows three Italians were killed, but by whom he does not know.

Chapter 13 — Impending Peril Forces Difficult Choices

The story of how Mrs. Isidor Straus, wife of the New York merchant, met death with her husband on the *Titanic* rather than be separated from him, was rendered complete when Miss Ellen Bird, maid to Mrs. Straus, told how the self-sacrifice of Mrs. Straus made it possible for her to escape a watery grave.

Miss Bird also supplied details of the appealing scenes between Mrs. Straus and her husband when the elderly, though heroic woman, brushed aside three opportunities to be saved, declaring to solicitous passengers that death in her husband's arms was more to be desired than life without him.

Miss Bird's narrative was repeated by Sylvester Byrnes, general manager of R.H. Macy & Co. According to Byrnes:

"When the *Titanic* struck the iceberg Mr. and Mrs. Straus were walking arm in arm on the upperdeck. Although assured by the officers that there was no immediate cause for alarm, Mrs. Straus, with her husband, hurried to the stateroom of her maid, cautioning Miss Bird to dress hurriedly and as comfortably as she could, because the passengers might have to take to the lifeboats. Then Mr. and Mrs. Straus returned to the deck, where, shortly after, they were joined by Miss Bird.

"Mr. Straus stepped aside when the first boat was being filled, explaining that he could not go until all the women and children had been given places. 'Where you are, Papa, I shall be,' said Mrs. Straus, rejecting all entreaties to enter the boat.

Into the Darkness

Emily Richards

Mrs. Emily Richards, who with her mother and her two children, was on the *Titanic*, journeying from Penzance, Cornwall, to join her husband in Akron, Ohio, said:

"I had put the children in bed and had gone to bed myself. We had been making good time all day, the ship rushing through the sea at a tremendous rate, and the air on deck was cold and crisp. I didn't hear the collision, for I was asleep. But my mother came and shook me.

"'There is surely danger,' said Mamma. 'Something has gone wrong.'

"So we put on our slippers and outside coats and got the children into theirs and went on deck. We had on our night gowns under our coats. As we went up the stairway someone was shouting down in a calm voice: 'Everybody put on their life preservers before coming on deck!'

"We went back and put them on, assuring each other that it was nothing. When we got on deck we were told to pass through the dining room to a ladder that was placed against the side of the cabins and led to the upper deck.

"We were put through the portholes into the boats, and the boat I was in had a foot of water in it. As soon as we were in we were told to sit down on the bottom. In that position we were so low that we could not see out over the gunwale.

"Once the boat had started away some of the women stood up, and the seamen, with their hands full with the oars, simply put their feet on them and forced them back into the sitting position.

Into the Darkness

"We had not got far away by the time the ship went down, and after that there were men floating in the water all around, and seven of them were picked up by us in the hours that followed between that and daybreak.

Richards continued. "Some of these seven were already mad with exposure, and babbled gibberish, and kept trying to get up and overturn the boat. The other men had to sit upon them to hold them down.

"Two of the men picked up were so overcome with the cold of the water that they died before we reached the *Carpathia*, and their dead bodies were taken aboard. One woman, who spoke a tongue none of us could understand, was picked up by the boat and believed that her children were lost.

"She was entirely mad. When her children were brought to her on the *Carpathia* she was wild with joy, and lay down on the children on the floor, trying to cover them with her body, like a wild beast protecting its young, and they had to take her children away from her for the time to save them from being suffocated."

Caroline Bonnell

Miss Caroline Bonnell, of Youngstown, Ohio, one of the survivors, said that passengers who got into lifeboats were led to believe that a steamship was near and that the lives of all would be saved.

Miss Bonnell and her aunt, Miss Lily Bonnell, of London, England, were traveling with George D. Wick, an iron and steel manufacturer of Youngstown, his wife and daughter, Mary Natalie Wick. The women were saved. Mr. Wick went down with the ship. Like hundreds of others, he stood aside to give the women and children first chance.

Into the Darkness

"Miss Wick and I occupied a stateroom together," said Miss Bonnell. "We were awakened shortly before midnight by a sudden shock, a grinding concussion. Miss Wick arose and looked out of the stateroom window. She saw some men playfully throwing particles of ice at one another, and realized that we had struck an iceberg.

"She and I dressed, not hastily, for we were not greatly alarmed, and went on deck.

"There we found a number of passengers. Naturally they were all somewhat nervous but there was nothing approaching a panic. The other members of our party also had come on deck, and we formed a little group by ourselves.

"We were told to put on life belts, and obeyed. Then the sailors began to launch the lifeboats. Still we were not alarmed. We had no doubt that all on board would be saved. In fact, we had no idea that the ship was sinking and believed that the resort to the lifeboats was merely a precaution.

"Mr. Wick kissed his wife good-by, and our boat, the first on that side of the ship, was lowered to the sea. There were about 25 women in the boat, with two sailors and a steward to row. These were the only men. The boat would have held many more"

Miss Bonnell continued: "As the boat was being loaded, the officer in charge pointed out a light that glowed dimly in the distance on the surface of the sea and directed our sailors to row to that, land their passengers and return to the *Titanic* for more.

"As we were rowed away we saw that the great liner was settling. We kept our boat pointed toward the light to which we were to row. As a matter of fact, there were two lights—one red and the other white. Sailormen on the *Carpathia* told us subsequently that the lights might have been those of a fishing boat caught in the ice and drifting with it—but who can tell?

"After a while our sailors ceased rowing, saying it was of no use to keep on. Then we women tried to row, with the double light our objective. We rowed and rowed, but did not seem to gain on the light, which, like a will-o'-the-wisp, seemed ever to evade us. Finally we gave up and sat huddled in the lifeboat.

"Some of the women complained of the cold, but the members of our own party did not suffer, being provided with plenty of wraps," Miss Bonnell said.

"From the distance of a mile or more we heard the explosion and saw the *Titanic* go down. The lights did not go out all at once. As the ship slowly settled the rows of lights, one after another, winked out, disappearing beneath the surface. Finally the ship plunged down, bow first, and the stern slipped beneath the waves.

"Even then we had hoped that all on board might be saved. It was only after we had been taken aboard the *Carpathia*, and somehow few of us there were compared with the great company aboard the *Titanic*, that we got the first glimmer of the appalling reality."

Alfred White

"I never dreamed that it was serious," said Alfred White, one of the two oilers from the engine room who were saved by being picked up.

"I was on the whale deck in the bow calling the watch that was to relieve me when the ice first came aboard. It was a black berg that we struck—that is, it was composed of black ice. It could not be seen at all at night.

"The striking opened seams below the water line, but did not even scratch the paint above the line. I know that because I was one of those who helped make an examination over the side with a lantern," White said.

"I went down into the light engine room, where my station was, at 12.40 o'clock. We even made coffee, showing that there wasn't much thought of danger. An hour later I was still working around the light engines. I heard the chief engineer tell one of his subordinates that No. 6 bulkhead had given away.

"At that time things began to look bad, for the *Titanic* was far down by the bow. I was told to go up and see how things were going, and made my way up through the dummy funnel to the bridge deck.

"By that time all the boats had left the ship and yet everyone in the engine room was at his post. I was near the captain and heard him say: 'Well, boys, I guess it's every man for himself now.'

"I slipped down some loose boat falls and dropped into the water. There was a boat not far away, which later picked me up. There were five firemen in her as a crew, 49 women and 16 children. There was no officer.

White continued: "During the six hours we were afloat we were near what we boys later called the millionaires' boat. That lifeboat had only sixteen passengers in her. When all were put aboard the *Carpathia* the six men who were the crew of that millionaires' boat each got £5. Those who had worked harder saving second-class passengers didn't get a cent."

White then told of the way in which the children from the open boats were swung aboard the *Carpathia* in sacks, while the women were hoisted up in rope swings.

"Near the boat in which I was," White went on, "were two collapsible boats, which had failed to work and were not better than rafts. They had 32 men clinging to them who were later picked up by the lifeboats.

"The other two collapsible boats, which had about 60 persons in them, deposited what women they carried in the regular lifeboats and went to the scene of the sinking.

"From the water were picked up perhaps 50 of the crew who had floated off when she sank or else who had jumped before. The second officer was picked up, too, and took command of a boat.

"Now, about the sinking itself. There was some sort of an explosion just about 2 o'clock, or shortly after I had gone overboard. It was not until this explosion, the nature of which I do not know, that the lights went out. They had been fed by steam from oil boilers."

White continued: "The explosion caused a break in the ship just aft of the third funnel. The forward section went down bow first. The after part then seemed almost to right itself, and we thought she might keep afloat.

"But it wasn't long before the propellers shot out of the water, and down she went. A steward who stood on the poop deck had the ship go down under him. He was picked up later, and his watch was found to have stopped at 2.20 A.M., so we knew that that was the time she foundered. There was no apparent suction when she foundered.

"While we were cruising about the place, our oars continually bumped into dead bodies, wearing life belts. Some of the bodies were of the half-naked stokers. They were killed by the shock. We knew that the temperature of the water had been 28 degrees at 11 o'clock the same evening. While we were waiting for the boat to go down we heard some fifteen or twenty shots from the rail of the ship. We only surmised what they were."

Chapter 14 — Survivors Recount Terrifying Final Moments

Lawrence Beesley, a Cambridge University man, who was a second-cabin passenger on the *Titanic*, amplified his previous account while visiting the White Star offices. After describing events immediately following the collision with the iceberg and his departure in a lifeboat, Mr. Beesley is quoted as saying:

"We drifted away easily once we got the oars out, and headed directly away from the ship. Our crew seemed to be mostly cooks in white jackets, two at an oar, with a stoker at the tiller, who had been elected captain. He told us he had been at sea 26 years and had never yet seen such a calm night on the Atlantic.

"As we rowed away from the *Titanic* we looked back from time to time to watch her, and a more striking spectacle it was not possible for anyone to see. In the distance, she looked an enormous length, her great bulk outlined in black against the starry sky, every porthole and saloon blazing with light. It was impossible to think anything could be wrong with such a leviathan, were it not for that ominous tilt downward in the bows where the water was by now up to the lowest row of portholes.

"About 2 a.m., as near as I can remember, we observed her settling very rapidly, with the bows and the bridge completely under water, and concluded it was now only a question of minutes before she went, and so it proved. She slowly tilted straight on end, with the stern vertically upward, and, as she did, the light in the cabins and saloons, which had not flickered for a moment since we left, died out, came on again for a single flash, and finally went out altogether.

"At the same time, the machinery roared down through the vessel with a rattle and a groaning that could be heard for miles, the weirdest sound, surely, that could be heard in the middle of the ocean a thousand miles away from land.

"But this was not quite the end. To our amazement, she remained in that upright position for a time which I estimate at five minutes; others in the boat say less, but it was certainly some minutes while we watched at least one hundred and fifty feet of the *Titanic* towering up above the level of the sea and looming black against the sky."

Beesley continued. "Then, with a quiet, slanting dive, she disappeared beneath the waters. And there was left to us the gently heaving sea, the boat filled to standing room with men and women in every conceivable condition of dress and undress; above, the perfect sky of brilliant stars, with not a cloud in the sky, all tempered with a bitter cold that made us all long to be one of the crew who toiled away with the oar.

"And then, with all these, there fell on the air the most appalling noise that ever human ear listened to—the cries of hundreds of our fellow-beings struggling in the icy-cold water, crying for help with a cry that we knew could not be answered. We longed to return and pick up some of those swimming, but this would have meant swamping our boat and further loss of the lives of all of us. We tried to sing to keep the women from hearing the cries, and rowed hard to get away from the scene of the wreck.

"We kept a lookout for lights, and several times it was shouted that steamers' lights were seen.

Presently, now down on the horizon, we saw a light that slowly resolved itself into a double light, and we watched eagerly to see if the two would separate and so prove to be only two of our boats. To our joy they moved as one, and round we swung the boat and headed for her.

"The steersman shouted: 'Now, boys, sing!' and for the first time the boat broke into song, 'Row for the Shore, Sailors,' and for the first time tears came to the eyes of us all as we realized that safety was at hand. Our rescuer showed up rapidly, and as she swung around we saw her cabins all alight, and knew she must be a large steamship. She was now motionless and we had to row to her. Just then day broke—a beautiful, quiet dawn. We were received with a welcome that was overwhelming in its warmth."

Into the Darkness

Almost frenzied by the memory of the disaster through which they had passed, many of the survivors were unable for days even to discuss all the details of the *Titanic* horror.

Lady Duff-Gordon

One of the more intriguing accounts was given by Lady Duff-Gordon, wife of Sir Cosmo Duff-Gordon, who dictated it. Her tale shows that the *Titanic* was near icebergs before she went to bed on the night of the disaster. Here is her story, as well as that of others:

"I was asleep. The night was perfectly clear. We had watched for some time the fields of ice. There was one just before I went below to retire. I noticed among the fields of ice a number of large bergs.

"There was one which one of the officers pointed out to me. He said that it must have been 100 feet high and seemed to be miles long. It was away off in the distance. I went to my bedroom and retired.

"I was awakened by a long grinding sort of shock. It was not a tremendous crash, but more as though some one had drawn a giant finger all along the side of the boat.

"I awakened my husband and told him that I thought we had struck something. There was no excitement that I could hear, but my husband went up on deck. He returned and told me that we had hit some ice, apparently a big berg, but that there seemed to be no danger. We went on deck."

Lady Duff-Gordon continued: "No one, apparently, thought there was any danger. We watched a number of women and children and some men going into the lifeboats. At last one of the officers came to me and said, 'Lady Gordon, you had better go in one of the boats.'

"I said to my husband: 'Well, we might as well take the boat, although I think it will be only a little pleasure excursion until morning.'

"The boat was the twelfth or thirteenth to be launched. It was the captain's special boat. There was still no excitement. Five stokers got in and two Americans—A.L. Solomon, of New York, and L. Stengel, of Newark. Besides these there were two of the crew, Sir Cosmo, myself and a Miss Frank, an English girl.

"There were a number of other passengers, mostly men, standing nearby and they joked with us because we were going out on the ocean. 'The ship can't sink,' said one of them. 'You will get your death of cold out there in the ice.'

"We were slung off and the stokers began to row us away. We cruised around among the ice for two hours. Sir Cosmo had looked at his watch when we went off. It was exactly 12.15 A.M., and I should think fifteen minutes after the boat struck. It did not seem to be very cold. There was no excitement aboard the *Titanic*.

"Suddenly I had seen the *Titanic* give a curious shiver. The night was perfectly clear. There was no fog, and I think we were a thousand feet away. Everything could be clearly seen. There were no lights on the boats except a few lanterns which had been lighted by those on board.

"Almost immediately after the boat gave this shiver we heard several pistol shots and a great screaming arose from the decks," Lady Duff-Gordon said.

"Then the boat's stern lifted in the air and there was a tremendous explosion. Then the *Titanic* dropped back again. The awful screaming continued. Ten minutes after this there was another explosion. The whole forward part of the great liner dropped down under the waves. The stern rose a hundred feet, almost perpendicularly. The boat stood up like an enormous black finger against the sky. The screaming was agonizing. I never heard such a continued chorus of utter despair and agony.

"Then there was another great explosion and the great stern of the *Titanic* sank as though a great hand was pushing it gently down under the waves. As it went, the screaming of the poor souls left on board seemed to grow louder. It took the *Titanic* but a short time to sink after that last explosion. It went down slowly without a ripple.

"We had heard the danger of suction when one of these great liners sink. There was no such thing about the sinking of the *Titanic*. The amazing part of it all to me as I sat there in the boat, looking at this monster being, was that it all could be accomplished so gently.

Into the Darkness

"Then began the real agonies of the night. Up to that time no one in our boat, and I imagine no one in any of the other boats, had really thought that the *Titanic* was going to sink. For a moment a silence seemed to hang over everything, and then from the water about where the *Titanic* had been arose a bedlam of shrieks and cries. There were women and men clinging to the bits of wreckage in the icy water."

Lady Duff-Gordon continued: "It was at least an hour before the last shrieks died out. I remember next the very last cry was that of a man who had been calling, loudly: 'My God! My God!' He cried monotonously, in a dull, hopeless way. For an entire hour there had been an awful chorus of shrieks gradually dying into a hopeless moan until this last cry that I spoke of. Then all was silent. When the awful silence came, we waited gloomily in the boats throughout the rest of the night.

"At last morning came. On one side of us was the ice floes and the big bergs, and oil. On the other side we were horrified to see a school of tremendous whales. Then, as the mist lifted, we caught sight of the *Carpathia* looming up in the distance and headed straight for us.

"We were too numbed by the cold and horror of that awful night to cheer or even utter a sound. We just gazed at one another and remained speechless. Indeed, there seemed to be no one among us who cared much what happened.

"Those in the other boats seemed to have suffered more than we had. We, it seemed, had been miraculously lucky. In one of the boats was a woman whose clothing was frozen to her body.

"The men on the *Carpathia* had to chop it off before she could be taken to a warm room. Several of the stokers and sailors who had manned the boats had been frozen to death, and they lay stiff and lifeless in the bottom of the boats, while the women and children were lifted to the *Carpathia*.

"I did not see Captain Smith after I was put into the small boat, but others told me that when the *Titanic* went down, Captain Smith was seen swimming in the icy water. He picked up a baby that was floating on a mass of wreckage and swam with it to one of the small boats. He lifted the baby into the boat, but the child was dead," Lady Duff-Gordon said.

"The women in the boat, according to the story told me, wanted the captain to get into the boat with them, but he refused, saying: 'No, there is a big piece of wreckage over here, and I shall stick to that. We are bound to be rescued soon.' Nothing more was seen of Captain Smith.

"There was an absolute calm and silence on the *Carpathia*. There were hundreds of women who had lost their husbands, and among them fifteen brides. Few of these had been married more than five or six months. No one cared to talk. The gloom was awful. I buried myself in my cabin and did not come on deck again."

Robert Hichens

From Robert Hichens—quartermaster at the wheel of the *Titanic* when the great vessel crashed into the iceberg, and then in command of one of the boats which left the steamship before it went down—have come details of the terrible sight at sea, which could have been known to perhaps no other person.

And standing out in memory of this young Cornishman are shrieks and groans that went up from the dark hulk of the giant steamship before she sank.

Into the Darkness

Hichens, a type of young Englishman who follows the sea, had for years been on the troopship *Dongolo*, running to Bombay, and thought himself fortunate when he obtained his berth as quartermaster of the *Titanic*, the greatest and largest of all steamships. He told in their sequence the events of the night and morning of April 14 and 15.

It was in his boat that Mrs. John Jacob Astor took her place, after Col. Astor had kissed her good-bye, and handed her a flask of brandy, then taking his place in the line of men, some of whom realized even then that the steamship was doomed. And his last sight as his boat was lowered was of Captain Smith, standing on the bridge, giving his orders as calmly as if he were directing her entrance into a harbor.

He told of how the officers stood with revolvers drawn, to enforce, if the emergency should arise, that rule of the sea of women first; but the emergency did not arise, and the men stood back or helped the women to their seats.

In the way of a seaman, he told the narrative of the night spent in the little boat, comforting as best he could the women who did not realize as he did that some of them had looked upon their loved ones for the last time.

"My watch was from 8 to 12 o'clock," said Hichens. "From 8 to 10 o'clock I was the stand-by man, and from 10 to 11 o'clock I had the wheel. When I was at the stand-by it was very dark, and, while it was not dark, there was a haze. I cannot say about the weather conditions after 10 o'clock, for I went into the wheelhouse, which is enclosed.

"The second officer was the junior watch officer from 8 to 10 o'clock, and at 8 o'clock, he sent me to the carpenter with orders for him to look after the fresh water, as it was going to freeze.

"The thermometer then read 31½ degrees, but so far as could be seen there was no ice in sight. The next order was from the second officer for the deck engineer to turn the steam on in the wheelhouse, as it was getting much colder. Then the second officer, Mr. Lightoller, told me to telephone the lookout in the crow's nest.

"'Tell them,' he said, 'to keep a sharp and strict lookout for small ice until daylight and to pass the word along to the other lookout men.

"I took the wheel at 10 o'clock, and Mr. Murdock, the first officer, took the watch. It was 20 minutes to 12, and I was steering when there were the three gongs from the lookout, which indicated that some object was ahead," Hichens said.

Into the Darkness

"Almost instantly, it could not have been more than four or five seconds, when the lookout men called down on the telephone, 'Iceberg ahead!' Hardly had the words come to me when there was a crash.

"I ain't likely to forget, sir, how the crash came. There was a light grating on the port bow, then a heavy crash on the port bow, then a heavy crash on the starboard side. I could hear the engines stop, and the lever closing the watertight emergency doors."

Hichens continued: "Mr. Murdock was the senior officer of the watch, and with him on the bridge were Mr. Buxtell, the fourth officer, and Mr. Moody, the sixth officer. The *Titanic* listed, perhaps, five degrees, to the starboard, and then began to settle in the water. I stood attention at the wheel from the time of the crash until 20 minutes after 12, and had no chance to see what the captain did."

H.E. Steffanson

H.E. Steffanson, of New York, another survivor who leaped into the sea and was picked up, declared that he saw the iceberg before the collision.

"It seemed to me that the berg, a mile away, I should say, was about 80 feet out of the water. The ice that showed clear of the water was not what we struck. After the collision I saw ice all over the sea. When we hit the berg we seemed to slide up on it. I could feel the boat jumping and pounding, and I realized that we were on the ice, but I thought we would weather it. I saw the captain only once after the collision. He was telling the men to get the women and children into the boats. I thought then that it was only for precaution, and it was long after the boats had left that I felt the steamer sinking.

"I waited on the upper deck until about 2 o'clock. I took a look below and saw that the *Titanic* was doomed. Then I jumped into the ocean and within five minutes I was picked up."

Steffanson also described the discipline upon the boat as perfect. Many women, as well as men, he said, declined to leave the *Titanic*, believing she was safe.

Cornelia Andrews

Miss Cornelia Andrews, of Hudson, N.Y., was one of the first to be put into a lifeboat.

"I saw the *Titanic* sink," she said. "I saw her blow up. Our little boat was a mile away when the end came, but the night was clear and the ship loomed up plainly, even at that distance. As our boat put off I saw Mr. and Mrs. Astor standing on the deck. As we pulled away they waved their hands and smiled at us. We were in the open boat about four hours before we were picked up."

E.W. Beans, a second-cabin passenger, was picked up after swimming in the icy water for 20 minutes. He, too, jumped into the sea after the boats were lowered.

"I heard a shot fired," said Beans, "just before I jumped. Afterward I was told a steerage passenger had been shot while trying to leap into a lifeboat filled with women and children."

Chapter 15 — The Grim Task of Recovery

The cable ship *Mackay-Bennett*, which had been sent out to recover as many as possible of the *Titanic*'s dead, reached her pier in the dockyard at Halifax, Nova Scotia, the nearest port, at 9.30 on the morning of April 30, almost exactly two weeks after the disaster.

Down the gangway to the pier in the sunlight of a perfect April day they carried 190 of those who had started forth on the maiden voyage of the biggest ship afloat.

In her quest, the *Mackay-Bennett* had found 306 of the *Titanic*'s dead, but only 190 were brought to shore. The rest, the 116, were buried at sea. And 57 of those 116 were among the identified dead.

Of those who were brought to shore, 60 lay unnamed at the curling rink on the edge of the town. It was believed that the 60 were all members of the *Titanic*'s crew, but the slender hope that their own dead might be among them sent many to the rink.

One of the sixty was a little baby girl. Five of them were women, but none of the women that were found were from the first cabin passengers. There was no hope that the body of Mrs. Straus was among them. There was practically no hope that Major Butt was among the unnamed sixty. The quest of the *Mackay-Bennett* bore greater results than were anticipated, and Capt. F. W. Lardner believed that his ship recovered about all of those who did not go down in the *Titanic*.

The search was continued over five days, sometimes with the ship drifting without success amid miles and miles of wreckage, tables, chairs, doors, pillows, scattered fragments of the luxury that was the White Star liner *Titanic*.

At other times the bodies were found close together, and once they saw more than a hundred that looked to the wondering crew of the *Mackay-Bennett* like a flock of sea gulls in the fog, so strangely did the ends of the life belts rise and fall with the rise and fall of the waves.

Those whose dead the *Mackay-Bennett* brought to shore came forward with their claims, and from the middle of the afternoon the rest of the day was filled with the steps of identification and the signing of many papers.

The first to be claimed was John Jacob Astor and for his death was issued the first "accidental drowning" death certificate of the hundreds who lost their lives in the wreck of the *Titanic*.

Into the Darkness

Sharp and distinct in all the tidings the *Mackay-Bennett* brought to shore, the fact stands out that 56 of those who were identified on board were recommitted to the sea. Of the 190 identified dead that were recovered from the scene of the *Titanic* wreck, only 130 were brought to Halifax.

This news, which was given out almost immediately after the death ship reached her pier, was a confirmation of the suspicion that in the last few days had seized upon the colony of those waiting here to claim their dead.

Yet it came as a deep, a stirring surprise. It stunned the White Star men who have had to direct the work from Halifax.

They had been confidently posting the names of the recovered as the wireless brought the news in from the Atlantic.

When the suspicion arose that some of the identified might have been buried at sea, the White Star people said that they did not know, but they were working on the assumption that Capt. Lardner would bring them all to port, and that only the unidentifiable had been recommitted to the sea.

Then they learned that the *Mackay-Bennett* had brought in 60 unidentified. The hallway of the curling rink where the dead were removed from the cable ship was thronged all afternoon with friends and relatives eager beyond expression to see those unnamed dead, but the attention of the embalmers was turned to those already identified, for whom the claimants were waiting. For the most part, the unidentified could not be viewed until the next morning.

One of them was thought to be Arthur White, a member of the *Titanic*'s crew.

Into the Darkness

The suspense was acute. Yet those who were most anxious for the tomorrow to come knew that hope was of the slenderest. They knew that the nameless 60 were almost all members of the crew. Capt. Lardner said that he was sure of it. He knew it by the clothes they wore.

As to the 57 identified dead that were buried at sea, the whole colony was stirred by pity that it had to be, and not a few wonder if it really had to be, a wonder fed by the talk of some of the embalmers. Yet few were immediately concerned; most of those in Halifax were waiting for men who sailed first cabin of the *Titanic*. It appears that only one of these was among the ones who were buried at sea. This was Frederick Sutton, of Philadelphia. The large majority were either members of the *Titanic*'s crew or steerage passengers.

Capt. Lardner defends recovery decisions

Of the 116 that Capt. Lardner thought best to return to the sea, he explained that the unidentified seemed unidentifiable, that the identified were too mutilated to bring to shore.

"Let me say first of all," he announced when the reporters gathered around him, "that I was commissioned to bring aboard all the bodies found floating, but owing to the unanticipated number of bodies found, owing to the bad weather and other conditions it was impossible to carry out instructions, so some were committed to the deep after service, conducted by Canon Hind."

Capt. Lardner explained that neither he nor any of his people had dreamed that so many of the *Titanic*'s dead would be found floating on the surface of the Atlantic.

Into the Darkness

It was more than his embalmer could handle, for, although the material for embalming 70 bodies, which was all that Halifax sent out with the *Mackay-Bennett*, was supplemented at sea by materials borrowed from the *Minia*, the number of dead so preserved for the return to shore was only 106.

He did not know how long he would have to stay at his grim work on the scene of the wreck. He did not know how long bad weather would impede the homeward voyage.

He did not know how long he could safely carry the multitude of dead. It seemed best to recommit some to the sea, and so on three different days, 116 were weighted down and dropped over the edge of the ship into the Atlantic.

Then rose the question as to why some were picked for burial at sea and others left on board to be brought home to the waiting families on shore. The reporters put the question to the Captain, and he answered it:

"No prominent man was recommitted to the deep. It seemed best to embalm as quickly as possible in those cases where large property might be involved. It seemed best to be sure to bring back to land the dead where the death might give rise to such questions as large insurance and inheritance and all the litigation.

"Most of those who were buried out there were members of the *Titanic*'s crew. The man who lives by the sea ought to be satisfied to be buried at sea. I think it is the best place. For my own part, I should be contented to be committed to the deep."

To emphasize the uncertainty of the task he directed, Capt. Lardner pointed silently to the forward hold, where an hour before those on the pier had seen the dead lying side by side on the floor, each in the wrapping of tarpaulin.

"They were ready for burial," the Captain said. "We had weights in them, for we didn't know when we should have to give them up."

To those who hoped to find their own among the unidentified in the curling ring the next day, Capt. Lardner held out little encouragement except the prospect that the quest of the *Minia* may result in a few more bodies being recovered. He believed that his own ship gathered in most of those who were kept afloat by the lifebelts.

Almost all of the rest, in his opinion, went down with the rush of waters that closed over the *Titanic*, driving them down in the hatchways and holding the dead imprisoned in the great wreck.

Survivors told of many pistol shots heard in those dark moments when the last lifeboats were putting off, and though the pier on the night the *Carpathia* landed was a stir with rumors of men shot down as they fought to save their lives, not one of the bodies that were recovered yesterday had any pistol shots, according to Capt. Lardner and the members of his crew.

The mutilations which marked so many were broken arms and legs and crushed skulls, where the living on the *Titanic* were swept against the stanchions by the onrush of the sea.

The little repair shop on the *Mackay-Bennett* was a treasure house when she came to port. Fifteen thousand dollars in money was found on the recovered bodies and jewelry that will be worth a king's ransom. One of the crew related his experience with one dead man whose pockets he turned inside out only to have 17 diamonds roll out in every direction upon the littered deck.

It was a little after 9.30 that the *Mackay-Bennett* was sighted by those waiting for her since the break of day. For it was in the chill of 6 o'clock on a Canadian Spring morning that the people began to assemble on the pier in the dockyard.

They were undertakers for the most part, mingling with the newspaper men who hurried to and fro between the water's edge and the little bell tent set up a few yards back to guard the wires that were to flash the news to the ends of the continent.

The somber arrival of the *Mackay-Bennett*

The friends and relatives of those who were lost when the great liner went down were urged not to assume the ordeal of meeting the *Mackay-Bennett*. Almost without exception they followed this advice, and only a scattering few could be seen among those waiting on the pier.

In all the crowd of men, officials, undertakers, and newspaper men, there was just one woman, solitary, spare, clasping her heavy black shawl tightly around her.

This was Eliza Lurette, for more than 30 years in the service of Mrs. William August Spencer, who was waiting at her home in New York, while Miss Lurette had journeyed to Halifax to seek the body of Mr. Spencer, who went down with the *Titanic*.

Into the Darkness

So the crowd that waited on the pier was made up almost entirely of men who had impersonal business there, and the air was full of the chatter of conjecture and preparation.

Then, warned by the tolling of the bells up in the town, a hush fell upon the waiting people. The gray clouds that had overcast the sky parted, and the sun shone brilliantly on the rippling water of the harbor as the *Mackay-Bennett* drew alongside her pier.

Capt. Lardner could be seen upon the bridge. The crew hung over the sides, joyously alive and glad to be home. But in every part of the ship the dead lay. High on the poop deck coffins and rough shells were piled and piled.

Dead men in tarpaulins lined the flooring of the cable-wells both fore and aft, so that there was hardly room for a foot to be put down. And in the forward hold, dead men were piled one upon another, their eyes closed as in sleep, and over them all a great tarpaulin was stretched. Those that pressed forward to see were sickened and turned back.

The business of the moment was to discharge that freight, and this was done with all possible dispatch. The uncoffined dead were carried down in stretchers, placed in the rough shells that were piled upon the pier, and one by one driven up the slope and into the town in the long line of hearses and black undertaker's wagons that had been gathered from every quarter. It was speedily done, but quietly and without irreverent haste.

For two hours this business proceeded before anyone could go upon the pier and the sounds were like the hum of a small factory. There were the muffled orders, the shuffling and tramping of feet, the scraping as of packing boxes drawn across the rough flooring and the eternal hammering that echoed all along the coal sheds.

Two hours it was before anyone could go on board, and then came another hour when the coffins were swung down from the deck and piled up on the wharf ready for the removal that took until well into the middle of the afternoon.

Few of the relatives were allowed to pass beyond the cordon that stretched all about the pier at which the dead were landed. One of the first to get through the lines and the first of all the waiting crowd to make his way aboard after the ship reached her pier was Capt. Richard Roberts, of the Astor yacht, who was filled with a great concern at the news that had come from the Widener party.

For long before the *Mackay-Bennett* reached her pier it was established as definitely as it may ever be established that the man who was picked up at sea for George D. Widener was not Mr. Widener, but his man-servant Edward Keating.

Although the name was sent in by wireless, a later examination of the dead man's clothing and effects proved that it was Keating's body. A letter in the pocket was addressed to Widener, but the coat was labeled "E.K." and the garments were of an inferior quality. Identification by features was out of the question, for the dead man had been struck by some spar or bit of wreckage, and the face was mutilated past recognition. He was buried at sea, and the news sent on to the waiting family.

Young Mr. Widener, who had been waiting here for a week with a private car to carry the body of his father home to Philadelphia, had heard of the uncertainty, and in a fever of impatience he met the *Mackay-Bennett* at Quarantine, went over the effects with Captain Lardner, and was satisfied that it was Keating whose body was found and who was later committed to the deep.

The haunting fear that this same error might have been made in the case of Colonel Astor had possession of the whole Astor party and grew acute as the Widener story went out. That was what sent Captain Roberts hurrying to the ship. He was admitted and saw for himself. The coffin top was removed.

The plain gold ring with the two little diamonds set deep, the gold buckle on the belt that Colonel Astor always wore, and a sum amounting to nearly $3,000 in the pockets settled the uncertainty. Twenty minutes after he had boarded the ship, Captain Roberts was hurrying through the crowd to reach the nearest telephone that he might speed the news to waiting Vincent Astor.

Beyond these two cases, the questions of identity were taken up at the Mayflower Curling Rink at the edge of the town, where the line of hearses had been trundling since the *Mackay-Bennett* landed. As they passed, the crowds were hushed, men bowed their heads, and officers saluted.

At the rink the great main floor was given over to the coffins and shells containing the identified dead, and as soon as the embalmers had done their work, the friends and relatives came forward and claimed their own.

Upstairs in the large, bare room the packets of clothing were distributed in rows upon the floor.

There the oak chests of the Provincial Cashier were opened for the sorting of the canvas bags that contained the valuables, the letters and the identifying trinkets of the dead. It was all very systematic. It was all very much businesslike, and while a lunch counter served refreshments to the weary workers, and while the Intercolonial set up a desk for railway tickets, the Medical Examiner was busy issuing death certificates, and the Registrar was issuing burial permits, all to the accompanying click, click of several typewriters.

A satisfactory arrangement was reached as to the disposition of the personal effects. A man would claim his dead, take the number, make his way to the representatives of the Provincial Secretary, and there claim the contents of the little canvas bag by making affidavit that he was the duly authorized representative of the executor or next of kin.

The little crimson tickets that are the death certificates were printed for the tragedies of every day in the year. Their formal points and dimensions seemed hopelessly inadequate for even the briefest statement of the tragedy of the *Titanic*.

Chapter 16 — Laid to Rest in the Cold, Calm Deep

After the greater part of the *Titanic*'s dead had been shifted from the *Mackay-Bennett* to the pier, Captain Lardner descended to the dining saloon, and with the reporters from all over the country gathered around the table, he opened the ship's log and, slowly tracing his fingers over the terse entries, he told them the story of the death ship's voyage.

Lardner is English by birth and accent, and tall and square of build, with a full brown beard and eyes of unusual keenness.

"We left Halifax," he began, "shortly after noon on Wednesday, April 17, but fog and bad weather delayed us on the run out, and we did not get there till Saturday night at 8 o'clock.

"We asked all ships to report to us if they passed any wreckage or bodies, and on Saturday at noon we received a communication from the German mailboat steamship *Rhein* to the effect that in latitude 42.1. N. longitude 49.13, she had passed wreckage and bodies, Captain Lardner said.

"The course was shaped for that position. Later in the afternoon we spoke to the German steamship *Bremen*, and they reported having passed three large icebergs and some bodies in 42 N. 49.20 W.

"We arrived on the scene at 8 o'clock Saturday evening, and then we stopped and let the ship drift. It was in the middle of the watch that some of the wreckage and a few bodies were sighted.

"At daylight the boats were lowered, and though there was a heavy sea running at the time, 51 bodies were recovered."

A solemn farewell at sea
The Rev. Canon K. C. Hinds, rector of All Saints' Cathedral, officiated at the burial of 116 bodies, the greatest number consigned to the ocean at one time.

Through the day some fifty were picked up. All were carefully examined and their effects placed in separate bags, all bodies and bags being numbered.

It was deemed wise that some of them should be buried. At 8 P.M. the ship's bell was tolled to indicate all was in readiness for the service. Standing on the bow of the ship as she rocked to and fro, one gazed at the starry heavens and across the boundless deep, and to his mind the psalmist's words came with mighty force.

"Whither shall I go then from Thy spirit, or whither shall I go then from Thy presence? If I ascend up to heaven Thou art there, I make my bed in the grave,

Thou art there also. If I take the wings of the morning and dwell in the uttermost part of the sea, even there shall Thy hand lead me, and Thy right hand shall hold me."

In the solemn stillness of the early night, the words of that unequaled burial office rang across the waters: "I am the resurrection and the life, saith the Lord. He that believeth in Me shall never die."

When the time of committal came these words were used over each body:

"Forasmuch as it hath pleased Almighty God to take up to Himself the soul of our dear brother departed, we, therefore, commit his body to the deep to be turned to corruption, looking for the resurrection of the body (when the seas shall give up her dead) and the life of the world to come, through Jesus Christ' Our Lord, who shall change

our vile body, that it may be like unto His glorious body, according to the mighty working whereby He is able to subdue all things to Himself."

The prayers from the burial service were said, the hymn "Jesus, Lover of My Soul," sung and the blessing given.

Any one attending a burial at sea will most surely lose the common impression of the awfulness of a grave in the mighty deep. The wild Atlantic may rage and toss, the shipwrecked mariners cry for mercy, but far below in the calm untroubled depth they rest in peace.

Rev. Canon K. C. Hinds continued the story: "On Monday the work began again early in the morning, and another day was spent in searching and picking up the floating bodies and at night a number were buried. On Tuesday the work was still the same until the afternoon, when the fog set in, and continued all day Wednesday.

"Wednesday was partly spent in examining bodies, and at noon a number were committed to the deep. Thursday came in fine and from early morning until evening the work went on. During the day word came that the cable ship *Minia* was on her way to help and would be near us at midnight.

"Early on Friday some more bodies were picked up. The captain then felt we had covered the ground fairly well and decided to start on our homeward way at noon. After receiving some supplies from the *Minia*, we bid good-bye and proceeded on our way.

"The *Mackay-Bennett* succeeded in finding 306 bodies, of which 116 were buried at sea, and one could not help feeling, as we steamed homeward, that of those bodies we had on board it would be well if the greater number of them were resting in the deep," the Reverend said.

"It is to be noted how earnestly and reverently all the work was done and how nobly the crew acquitted themselves during a work of several days, which meant a hard and trying strain on mind and body.

"What seems a very regrettable fact is that in chartering the *Mackay-Bennett* for this work, the White Star Company did not send an official agent to accompany the steamer in her search for the bodies."

Into the Darkness

The story of the *Titanic* and its ill-fated maiden voyage still holds a special place in the public eye.

Chapter 17 — Forever Etched Into History

Some of the survivors wrote books so that the world would never forget *Titanic* or her last night.

The first books came from Archibald Gracie, who died before "The Truth About the *Titanic*" was published, and second class passenger Lawrence Beesley, who in "The Loss of the *Titanic*" wrote that, "No living person should seek to dwell in thought for one moment on such a disaster except in the endeavor to glean from it knowledge that will be of profit to the whole world in the future. When such knowledge is practically applied in the construction, equipment and navigation of passenger steamers—and not until then—will be the time to cease to think of the *Titanic* disaster and of the hundreds of men and women so needlessly sacrificed."

Others kept in touch through letters or meetings. Gladys Cherry, who along with her cousin the Countess of Rothes, left *Titanic* in Lifeboat 8, later wrote to Able Seaman Thomas Jones that "The dreadful regret I shall always have, and I know you share with me, is that we ought to have gone back to see whom we could pick up; but if you remember, there was only an American lady, my cousin, self and you who wanted to return."

The *Titanic* haunted her surviving officers, none of whom ever received their own commands, perhaps a consequence of their association with the most famous of shipwrecks.

The wreck was something most *Titanic* survivors preferred not to talk about, even to relatives. Most of those who were children in 1912 only began to speak of the disaster late in life. Those who did speak became star guests at events sponsored by the *Titanic* Historical Society.

They have gone—and we must commemorate the disaster without them, but each life saved contains a lesson for the world.

-END-

20 interesting *Titanic* facts

- The ship was loaded with only enough lifeboats to hold half of the *Titanic* passengers. There were 20 of them with a total capacity of 1,178 people; many lifeboats were lowered to the waters only half-full.
- Further facts on the *Titanic* indicate that the ship received information earlier regarding the presence of ice floes in the vicinity, yet continued to speed full throttle ahead towards tragedy.
- Among the property reported as lost on the *Titanic* were over 3,000 bags of mail and an automobile.
- Each first class passenger paid a whopping $4,350 for a parlor suite ticket and $150 for a berth ticket.
- The ship contained a heated swimming pool, a first for any sailing vessel.

Into the Darkness

- The ship was still so brand new when passengers boarded it on April 10th, 1912 that some of the paint was still wet.
- Every stateroom contained electric lighting and heat.
- Of the 1,517 people who perished in the sinking of the *Titanic*, only 306 bodies were recovered.
- The largest percentage of survivors came from first class passengers.
- Even though directions have been given for women and children to board the lifeboats first, a number of men were reported as survivors while a surprisingly large number of women and children perished in the disaster. Most of the women and children lost in the sinking came from second and third class.

Into the Darkness

- Sadly, Captain Smith had made plans to retire after seeing the *Titanic* safely across the Atlantic on her maiden voyage.
- It cost $7.5 million to build the *Titanic*.
- It took three years to fully construct the ship.
- Among the provisions when the *Titanic* set sail in Southampton, England were 40,000 eggs, 75,000 pounds of fresh meat and 1,000 bottles of wine.
- The *Titanic*'s total capacity was 3,547 passengers plus crew.
- The *Titanic*'s weight fully loaded was 46,328 tons.
- The *Titanic* was 882 feet/268 meters long.
- There were 29 boilers on board of the ship.
- The ship consumed 825 tons of coal in one day.
- The top speed of the *Titanic* was 23 knots.

Another intriguing factoid

When the *Titanic* began sending out distress signals, the *Californian*, rather than the *Carpathia*, was the closest ship; yet the *Californian* did not respond until it was much too late to help. At 12:45 a.m. on April 15th, crew members on the *Californian* saw mysterious lights in the sky (the distress flares sent up from the *Titanic*) and woke up their captain to tell him about it.

Unfortunately, the captain issued no orders. Since the ship's wireless operator had already gone to bed, the *Californian* was unaware of any distress signals from the *Titanic* until the morning, but by then the *Carpathia* had already picked up all the survivors. Many people believe that if the *Californian* had responded to the *Titanic*'s pleas for help, many more lives could have been saved.

Quotes from *Titanic* survivors

"What do you think I am? Do you believe that I'm the sort that would have left that ship as long as there were any women and children on board? That's the thing that hurts, and it hurts all the more because it is so false and baseless. I have searched my mind with deepest care, I have thought long over each single incident that I could recall of that wreck. I'm sure that nothing wrong was done; that I did nothing that I should not have done. My conscience is clear and I have not been a lenient judge of my own acts." — **J. Bruce Ismay, Director of the White Star Line**

"There was peace and the world had an even tenor to its way. Nothing was revealed in the morning the trend of which was not known the night before. It seems to me that the disaster about to occur was the event that not only made the world rub its eyes and awake, but woke it with a start and kept it moving at

a rapidly accelerating pace ever since, with less and less peace, satisfaction and happiness. To my mind the world of today awoke April 15th, 1912." — **Jack B. Thayer, *Titanic* Survivor**

"When anyone asks how I can best describe my experience in nearly 40 years at sea, I merely say, uneventful. Of course, there have been winter gales, and storms and the like, but in all my experience, I have never been in any accident of any sort worth speaking about. I never saw a wreck and never have been wrecked, nor was I ever in any predicament that threatened to end in disaster of any sort. You see, I am not very good material for a story" — **Captain Edward J. Smith, Commander of *Titanic***

"Many brave things were done that night but none more brave than by those few men playing minute after minute as the ship settled quietly lower and

lower in the sea—the music they played serving alike as their own immortal requiem and their right to be recorded on the rolls of undying fame." — **Lawrence Beesley, *Titanic* Survivor**

"To my poor fellow-sufferers: My heart overflows with grief for you all and is laden with sorrow that you are weighed down with this terrible burden that has been thrust upon us. May God be with us and comfort us all." — **Eleanor Smith, wife of the late Captain Smith**

"Come at once, we have struck a berg, it's a CQD old man." — **Jack Phillips, Wireless Operator**

"Icebergs loomed up and fell astern and we never slackened. It was an anxious time with the Titanic's fateful experience very close in our minds. There were 700 souls on Carpathia and those lives as well as the survivors of the Titanic herself depended on

the sudden turn of the wheel." — **Captain Arthur H. Rostron, Commander of *Carpathia***

"There is no danger that Titanic will sink. The boat is unsinkable and nothing but inconvenience will be suffered by the passengers." — **Phillip Franklin, White Star Line Vice-President**

"We do not care anything for the heaviest storms in these big ships. It is fog that we fear. The big icebergs that drift into warmer water melt much more rapidly under water than on the surface, and sometimes a sharp, low reef extending two or three hundred feet beneath the sea is formed. If a vessel should run on one of these reefs half her bottom might be torn away." — **Captain Edward J. Smith, Commander of *Titanic***

"My friend Clinch Smith made the proposition that we should leave and go toward the stern. But there

arose before us from the decks below a mass of humanity several lines deep converging on the boat deck facing us and completely blocking our passage to the stern. There were women in the crowd as well as men and these seemed to be steerage passengers who had just come up from the decks below. Even among these people there was no hysterical cry, no evidence of panic. Oh the agony of it." — **Colonel Archibald Gracie, *Titanic* Survivor**

"When day broke, I saw the ice I had steamed through during the night. I shuddered, and could only think that some other hand than mine was on that helm during the night." — **Captain Arthur H. Rostron, Commander of *Carpathia***

"The oarsman laid on their oars and all in the lifeboat were motionless as we watched her in absolute silence. Save some who would not look and

buried their heads on each other's shoulders." — **Lawrence Beesley, *Titanic* Survivor**

"About this time people began jumping from the stern, my friend Milton Long and myself stood beside each other and jumped on the rail. We did not give each other any messages for back home cause neither thought we would ever get back." — **Jack B. Thayer, *Titanic* Survivor**

"Striking the water was like a thousand knives being driven into one's body. The temperature was 28 degrees, four degrees below freezing." — **Charles Lightoller, Second Officer aboard *Titanic***

"The sounds of people drowning are something that I cannot describe to you, and neither can anyone else. It's the most dreadful sound and there is a

terrible silence that follows it." — **Eva Hart,** *Titanic* **Survivor**

"The partly filled lifeboat standing by about 100 yards away never came back. Why on Earth they never came back is a mystery. How could any human being fail to heed those cries." — **Jack B. Thayer,** *Titanic* **Survivor**

"Then creeping over the edge of the sea we saw a single light and presently a second below it. It seemed almost too good to be true and I think everyone's eyes were filled with tears, men's as well as women's. All around us we heard shouts and cheers." — **Lawrence Beesley,** *Titanic* **Survivor**

"At 8:30 all the people were on board. I wanted to hold a service, a short prayer of thankfulness for those rescued and a short burial service for those who were lost. While they were holding the service I

maneuvered around the scene of the wreckage. We saw nothing but one body." — **Captain Arthur H. Rostron, Commander of *Carpathia***

"I still think about the 'might have beens' about the Titanic—that's what stirs me more than anything else. Things that happened that wouldn't have happened if only one thing had gone better for her. If only, so many 'if onlys.' If only she had enough lifeboats. If only the watertight compartments had been higher. If only she had paid attention to the ice that night. If only the Californian did come. It becomes a haunting experience to me— it's the haunting experience of 'if only'." — **Walter Lord, *Titanic* historian and author**

"You weren't there at my first meeting with Ismay. To see the little red marks all over the blueprints. First thing I thought was: 'Now here's a man who wants me to build him a ship that's gonna be sunk.' We're sending gilded egg shells out to sea." —

Thomas Andrews, Managing Director of Harland and Wolff Shipyards

"My mother had a premonition from the very word 'GO.' She knew there was something to be afraid of and the only thing that she felt strongly about was that to say a ship was unsinkable was flying in the face of God. Those were her words." — **Eva Hart, *Titanic* Survivor**

"You could actually walk miles along the decks and passages covering different ground all the time. I was thoroughly familiar with pretty well every type of ship afloat, but it took me 14 days before I could, with confidence, find my way from one part of that ship to another." — **Charles Lightoller, Second Officer aboard *Titanic***

"Each night the sun sank right in our eyes along the sea, making an undulating glittering pathway, a

golden track charted on the surface of the ocean, which our ship followed unswervingly until the sun dipped below the edge of the horizon, and the pathway ran ahead of us faster than we could steam and slipped over the edge of the skyline — as if the sun had been a golden ball and had wound up its thread of gold too quickly for us to follow." — **Lawrence Beesley, *Titanic* Survivor**

"What impressed me at the time that my eyes beheld the horrible scene was a thin light-gray smoky vapor that hung like a pall a few feet above the broad expanse of sea that was covered with a mass of tangled wreckage. That it was a tangible vapor, and not a product of my imagination, I feel well assured. It may have been caused by smoke or steam rising to the surface around the area where the ship had sunk. At any rate it produced a supernatural effect. Add to this, within the area described, which was as far as my eyes could reach,

there arose to the sky the most horrible sounds ever heard by mortal man except by those of us who survived this terrible tragedy. The agonizing cries of death from over a thousand throats, the wails and groans of the suffering, the shrieks of the terror-stricken and the awful gasping for breath of those in the last throes of drowning, none of us will ever forget to our dying day." — **Colonel Archibald Gracie, *Titanic* Survivor**

"Let the truth be known, no ship is unsinkable. The bigger the ship, the easier it is to sink her. I learned long ago that if you design how a ship will sink, you can keep her afloat. I proposed all the watertight compartments and the double hull to slow these ships from sinking. In that way, you get everyone off. There's time for help to arrive, and the ship's less likely to break apart and kill someone while she's going down." — **Thomas Andrews, Managing Director of Harland and Wolff Shipyards**

Made in the USA
Monee, IL
06 February 2025

11710616R00187